Ethnologia Europaea

Journal of European Ethnology

Volume 36:2
2006

MUSEUM TUSCULANUM PRESS · UNIVERSITY OF COPENHAGEN

Copyright © 2007   Ethnologia Europaea, Copenhagen
Printed   in Sweden by Grahns Tryckeri AB, Lund 2007
Cover and layout   Pernille Sys Hansen
Cover photo   A Danish couple lying on the beach at Patong in Thailand. They will continue their vacation in Thailand, even though large areas have been destroyed after the recent tsunami. Reversed left-right. Polfoto, Martin Lehmann, 31.12.2004.
ISBN 978 87 635 0756 1
ISSN 0425 4597

This journal is published with the support of the Nordic board for periodicals in the humanities and social sciences.

Museum Tusculanum Press
University of Copenhagen
Njalsgade 126
DK-2300 Copenhagen S
www.mtp.dk

CONTENTS

Britta Timm Knudsen
Emotional Geography. Authenticity, Embodiment and Cultural Heritage   5

Ruth-Elisabeth Mohrmann
Anniversaries and Jubilees. Changing Celebratory Customs in Modern Times   16

Anneli Palmsköld
The Meaning of Weaving. Textiles in a Museum Magazine   26

Gisela Welz and Eva Maria Blum
Contested Modernities. Politics, Culture and Urbanisation in Portugal.
A Case Study from the Greater Lisbon Area   36

Gebhard Fartacek
The Outsider's Gaze as Part of the Methodological Toolkit?
Reflections on the Research Project the "Musikantenstadl"   54

Dani Schrire
The Camino de Santiago. The Interplay of European Heritage and New Traditions   69

EMOTIONAL GEOGRAPHY
Authenticity, Embodiment and Cultural Heritage

Britta Timm Knudsen

The intention in this article is to propose an alternative to the modernist structural manner of referring to and representing the Holocaust. The alternative is based on performative paradigms in tourist research and on the reading of Peter Eisenmann's Memorial to the Murdered Jews of Europe, a cultural heritage site in the center of Berlin. In places of remembrance such as Auschwitz-Birkenau the place is the scene of the crime but in the emotional geography of Peter Eisenmann the visitor experiences a cool authenticity, a light physical inscription in the cultural heritage. Contrary to the consuming of places which the gazing tourist perform the witnessing visitor invests bodily in this place and this investment becomes the coin of exchange with the past.

Keywords: Holocaust tourism, witnessing, body-investment, cool authenticity

Places mean a lot to us as individuals. We were born there, we went to school there, we met the love of our life there, and our grandparents have lived there all their lives. In other words, the site seems per se to hold the phenomenological perspective of embodiment and place. More complex entities, such as nations, also have places as important components in their own construction of the nation, often the sites of important battles, whether defeats or victories. Cognitively seen, we can partake in various relationships with our surroundings: we can sense them, imagine them, or understand them (Sartre 1940). Memory is inscribed in the sensing – or more radically: memory is necessary if we are to sense reality at all (Rosset 1985; Ricoeur 2000). But likewise, the meeting with the world is mixed with our conceptions of the world, more imaginary images tied to the fact that we see the world as we want to see it (Storey 2003). In other words, Sartre's tripartition never appears in a pure form, but always in specific combinations. Previous conceptions, memories, and wishful thinking mix with our sensed impression of the world.

When we attempt to describe places' importance, the attempt is often linked to their ability to make us remember the past, bring it forth as something we remember (the memorial, the monument), and in that memory, more or less mythologizing elements can appear. The war monuments found in any city with respect for itself are excellent sites in or around which the past is (re)constructed and the future of the nation is built – often in a mythological light. The traces of the past, of course, vary. Ricoeur says that the past is material, since it can be traced in the landscape, and also that it is immaterial, since it can be traced in the human mind, for instance as the impression of affect. In this article, I will focus on the indexical formation of traces. In classical Peircean semiotics, an indexical sign is a sign closely related to that which it represents (smoke from fire). But rather than point to the referent, indexicality can also be about the effect (pragmatic or emotional) that a text, a work or a phenomenon has on someone (Barthes 1983; Knudsen & Thomsen 2002). This article will focus on material traces that are indexical in both senses of the word.

In German there is a distinction between different types of memorials to the past. A *Denkmal* (memorial) is a place that symbolically brings to mind the past, meaning that the place has been designated in the present to *represent* the past in certain ways, such as in the form of a monument. An *Erinnerungsort* (a place of remembrance) can also be a monument, but it is a monument specific to that place, because it cannot be anywhere else. Here, the place stands in an indexical relationship to the referent, in that *the place must be the scene of the crime* in order to perform this function. An Erinnerungsort does not so much represent as *present* a past that calls forth definite reactions in those who experience such places. A third term, a *Mahnmal* (a warning memorial), is meant to remind us of the past in a certain way: it must be ethically appealing, relevant to a negative historical legacy. An Erinnerungsort and a Denkmal can thus also be a Mahnmal.

The Nature of the Trace – An Analysis of Signs

The monument for the American soldiers fallen in Vietnam, *The National Vietnam Veterans Memorial in Washington D.C.*, called The Wall, which was unveiled in 1984, is a Denkmal and a Mahnmal for the Vietnam War. Theoretically it could have been placed anywhere, but is situated in Washington, and as such in the official capital, far from the actual crime scenes, but close to the centre of politics. On the monumental black wall are 1,050 names of Americans fallen. The wall has a smooth, shiny surface, and the sober minimalism invites distanced, aesthetic contemplation – totally in the spirit of aesthetic sensibility prevalent in the 1980s. The Vietnam monument interpellates the viewer to ethical reflection via aesthetic distance in the Kantian sense.

In contrast, we have the Holocaust Museum and the Auschwitz-Birkenau monument as Erinnerungsort and Mahnmal in that it is both a monument to the past, but also the scene of the crime, where the atrocities of the past took place, so that the ethnical interpellation is exceedingly present here.

Auschwitz-Birkenau was added to Unesco's list of World Heritage sites in 1979. The cultural heritage here is composed of the painful memories in the heart of Europe.

As a memorial, Auschwitz-Birkenau is an indexical sign that documents itself as place. The symbolic plenty of the site is closely linked to its materiality and its ability to document and bear witness as an indexical sign. The site **is** a trace in itself, and a trace that has both iconic and symbolic manifestation. The site has – bar none – authenticity (Lowenthal 1985).

A European variant of the Washington Wall monument is Peter Eisenmann's *Memorial to the Murdered Jews of Europe*, which was commissioned in 1999 and unveiled in May, 2005. The memorial is located in the heart of Berlin, close to Brandenburger Tor, the German parliament, Joseph Goebbel's villa, Adolf Hitler's chancellery, and underground, the bunker where Hitler shot himself on April 20 1945 – adding a *metonymical proximity* to that which the memorial represents. This is an important point, both in relation to the authenticity of the memorial, but also in relation to the form of experience that the memorial allows. The memorial exists as a space that one can enter, be in for a period of time, and leave again – an affect-space where one can participate in a dialogue with the past based on the body's reaction to the environment.

In other words, both monuments have a symbolic relationship with that which they represent, but there are distinct differences in the monuments' visual impression, and thus the experience of the tourist at the monuments is very different. There have been a number of significant shifts in aesthetic and cultural sensibilities concerning the relationship between ethics and aesthetics, which we can use the Berlin monument to understand, but we can also use them to aid in a reading of the monument that raises it above its weighty modernistic heritage.

I deliberately use the designation "tourist" for the visitors to these historical monuments. With it, I want to point out two things. There is an extensive theme-tourism to crime-scenes ("blacks spots" or "sensation sights", Rojek 1997: 62), and also, the designation "tourist" actualises reflection on the relationship between the tourist-gaze's aesthetic consumption of sites (Urry 1990), and the ethical appeal emitted by Mahnmal sites.

Holocaust Tourism[1]

Every year, 700,000 tourists/pilgrims visit the site of Auschwitz, and six million people each year visit the museums in Amsterdam, Dachau, Jerusalem, Los Angeles, Oświęcim and Washington (Cole 1999: 113). With the Jewish museums in Berlin and Copenhagen and Eisenmann's great monument, the number of visitors far exceeds those who, through their families, were directly involved in the extermination of the Jews. Thus there is what one might call a cultural heritage's mass-tourism to these *Erinnerungsorte, Denkmäler and Mahnmale*, a cultural heritage's tourism that seeks the very traumatic core of the European past.

The juxtaposition of the Holocaust and mass tourism implies a representational-ethical problem long insisted upon by cultural theorists, literary scholars, and historians (Felman & Laub 1992; Friedlander 1992; Lyotard 1988; Sandbye 2001; Pollock 2005). For these theorists, the point is that the Holocaust on the one hand must be remembered by following generations, and on the other hand, that the Holocaust as event is so genuine that it can only be represented with difficulty. In other words, the Holocaust is an event we can barely allow ourselves to represent, because every representation or putting into words implies a hackneying or a profanation. Among other things, that was the lesson learned from the linguistically critical viewpoint of the 1950s and 60s, as it was expressed in French modernism (Duras, Beckett), and by Danish modernists like Villy Sørensen. One might counter by pointing out that some media (such as the photo: Sandbye) are better or more considerate with respect to representing the indescribable, but the point is that the ethical dilemma is expressed via a – let us call it – ban on representation. A ban on representation that can lead to a mythologizing of the event.

Dominick LaCapra (1998) is very precise when he points out that this type of logic contributes to canonising the event by surrounding it with a ban on images like the Jewish ban on pictures. Operating with the indescribable in the very core of this problem area is to make the monstrosity of the event into a general figure around the limits of representation. LaCapra is extremely sceptical about the reading of this historically specific trauma as a *structural* phenomenon, and as a kind of symbol for modernism (and by the way, it is Adorno, if anyone, who has canonised this way of interpreting the event). LaCapra finds such mythologizing destructive with regard to a historical understanding of the event, and to more context-dependent readings of forms of representation, a cause that I also plead here.

Another criticism of the mythologizing of Auschwitz concerns the unavoidable *fictionalising* of the event by its mythologizing. Tim Cole (1999) expresses the fear that the place is thus made vulnerable to attacks on its documentary truth value. When places are mythologized, they clearly acquire fictional status, thus losing documentary terrain in people's consciousness. Despite what one might think, it becomes more possible to deny the Holocaust when it is mythologized.

Apart from mythologizing, the documentary impulse of the site lies in very concrete relics belonging to the victims of the extermination of the Jews. Suitcases with labels from earlier travels, piles of shoes, hair, prized belongings – all relics with great authenticity, but objects doomed to decay, according to Cole. If the relics are to act as proof of the authenticity of the event, then the Holocaust as symbolic site is doomed to vanish as the things decay. Cole's argument is thus double: on the one hand, he warns against too violent a mythologizing of the event, on the other hand, he warns against too much dependence on perishable relics.[2]

In his work, Eisenmann goes beyond these two points of view, which point out the criticisable in a form of representation that views the Holocaust as a structural figure out of context, and which is on the lookout for fictionalisation as well as too great a dependence on perishable proofs.

The Hunger for Reality

The concept of hunger for reality is central to a characteristic of aesthetic sensibility at the turn of the century (Knudsen & Thomsen 2002). The 1990s, or some say the entire twentieth century (Žižek 2002), has suffered from the hunger for reality, both in the field of politics as well as in the desire to realise the fantasy image (Nazism), in the field of art through the will of the avant-garde to let art and life merge, or as a "passionate worship of the real" (Žižek 2002; Foster 1996) in a number of fields. The will for reality often results precisely in the limits of what can be spoken and sensed becoming the object of aesthetic attention. Therefore the interest in traumas, whether personal or collective, in art, culture, and politics has been enormous throughout the 90s.

With the trauma, the limits of what can be said and sensed are touched on; with the trauma, reality towers up as precisely *the real*. Interest in reality as a passionate worshiping of the real is a way of presenting *the irrefutable evidence of testimony* on the world. Interest in the eyewitness (Ellis 2002) or testimony on the whole (Felman & Laub 1992; Caruth 1995; Ricoeur 2000) both in artistic practices (Knudsen 2003 a) and in general, for instance in reporting the news, in documentaries etc., is an expression of the fact that accounts from "the edge of life" where bodies and the mental apparatus are in more or less danger (Knudsen 2003 b). These testimonies can be regarded as weighty, because we as observers can see events as affective and physical traces in the descriptions by the witnesses.

These phenomena re-actualise the need to think the phenomenologically sensing body as a body with competences and capacities beyond language. So in itself there is not necessarily any conflict in directly interpellating the body affectively and ethically.

We can say that there are three layers/levels at play that are of interest in the trauma as the core of personal and collective identities. There is a *documentary-referential* level, that treats the irrefutable truth value of that which is described (catastrophic eyewitness stories, as seen with Sept. 11, the Tsunami in South-East Asia, the Beslan hostage affair, Hurricane Katrina in the US). The second level treats *the traces left in the soul* by the traumatic events. Events must be experienced by *someone* in order to be traumatic, and the trauma can be seen and heard in faces and voices. In that way, the viewer is also activated morally and emotionally (Boltanski 1999; Chouliaraki 2003; Knudsen 2004). Victims and observers are linked in what we might call an affective fellowship.

The third level could be called the *pragmatic effects* of the trauma, or its context-related meaning. Obviously this is a question of different interpretations of the cultivation of limits. The cultivation of limits was an expression of linguistic criticism or linguistic scepticism in France in the 1950s and 60s (symptomatically expressed in Barthe's famous comment on the language as Fascist!). In the 90's valorising of both individual and collective traumas, there is no question of a frontal attack on the symbolic order. Rather it is a question of its limits being thematised in order for it to be re-established. The victims ask to be re-inscribed in a relationship that has momentarily been broken, and the witnesses again validate this re-establishment of a contract and confirm it in the hearing of others. In other words, a re-establishment of a contract of fellowship.

The first level treats the relationship of the representation to the referential level (truth), the second level is concerned with whether the victims are able to affect the witnesses emotionally, and the third level is concerned with reciprocal acknowledgment and the establishment of new contracts between victim and witness. On the last level, we find ourselves in the witness's practice and pragmatic use of the phenomena.

Before turning to Eisenmann's memorial, it would be advantageous to look at how theoretical literature on tourism has gone from thematising the relationship between tourist and destination as a balance of power to thematising it as a bodily state.

Tourism, Gaze and Body

The tourist experience in Auschwitz has been described as follows in *Images of the Holocaust*: "We were tourists of guilt and righteousness: guilt at an almost pornographic sense of expectancy of the voyeurism ahead. And yet guilt tempered by a sense of righteousness at choosing to come to this place" (Cole 1999: 97). According to Cole, elements of the emotions linked to the Holocaust-tourist experience are righteousness and guilty voyeuristic greed at the prospect of the chamber of horrors that Auschwitz is to us descendants.

The feeling of guilt refers to the voyeurism, but also to the fundamental fact that it emanates from a body that is safe from the threat of death permanently hanging over the inmates of Auschwitz. Urry (1990) has thematised the tourist's gaze as analogous to the doctor's gaze at a patient, a gaze with the power to diagnose the patient in relation to a specific professional knowledge, and which places the patient in an inferior and subservient position as one who is being gazed upon. Urry thematises the relationship between the tourist and the locality as a structural relationship between One and the Other.

In continuation of Dean MacCannell's (1976) thematising of the western tourist's longing for originality and authenticity as a reflection of modern life's lack of these things, Urry operates with the tourist bringing his preconceptions with him from home, and these are not changed or tested by the tourist experience. Modern tourism's indubitably increased degree of mediatisation to some degree confirms this ethnocentric figure, so that "a circular confirmation of self-identity" (Jackson 2005: 191) is implicated. Mediaisation – through the Internet, TV, and films – can easily contribute to maintaining a specific gaze on the world in spite of increased mobility, both virtually and physically.

The Tsunami photo which is the cover illustration of this issue of *Ethnologia Europaea* was named News Photo of the year 2004, and was taken by photographer Martin Lehmann and published in the Danish newspaper *Politiken*. The photo can help us formulate some fundamental changes in the understanding of tourism, the gaze, and power; changes that have taken place since Urry's book from 1990. Since it was published, there has been a performative shift in tourism-research (Bærenholdt et al. 2004). The modern tourist experience is no longer thematised solely as a visual phenomenon, but as a *bodily investment in a place* (Crouch & Lübbren 2003).

This picture can be seen as a perfect echo of Holocaust-tourism's feelings of guilt over being in the place where such horrific things have happened, coupled with self-righteousness at having chosen this place. Of course, we cannot know what motive the tourists in the picture have for being there, or more correctly, for remaining there, in this post-catastrophic place, but the result of their remaining can clearly be seen. We can say that the picture shows both local inhabitants and visitors in the same frame as being the same, yet different. The catastrophe showed that both groups are potential victims, precisely because of their physical presence at the site, but there is a clear degree of difference in the victim-state, depending on whether the site is "home" or an exotic foreign destination.

On one level, the picture can be interpreted as the total triumph of western, ethnocentric tourism. Here lie three self-satisfied westerners, fully absorbed in their own holiday project, completely lacking any form of sensitivity to the suffering of others. Despite the fact that the place shows clear traces of the catastrophe, and thus takes on the character of a concrete "vulnerable" place, the tourists insist the place – as a mental projection of their own desires – still be the holiday paradise they originally came here to enjoy. In this interpretation, the balance of power is unambiguous. The western tourist's search for exotic authenticity (which is a mythologizing of people and places) does not allow itself to be corrected by "petty" considerations of the intrusion of reality into his or her holiday paradise.

In a reading of the balance of power in pact with Urry's thoughts from *The Tourist Gaze*, the two representatives of the local inhabitants are the staged "victims" in the tourist's own narrative. But the two inhabitants, turning their faces to the camera, are smiling. Without denying that there is a balance of power in the relationship between the tourist and the local inhabitants, the body language expresses conscious demeanour.

Whether or not the smile means that the local inhabitants are "playing the part" of happy, service-minded tourist-servants (i.e. playing the part in a staged authenticity (MacCannell 1976)), or it is the expression of a "smile, you're on" attitude, or more likely, it is a commentary grin at the grotesque sight that meets the viewer (the photographer, us), the smile is an expression of a consciousness of the role that partly lifts the smiling persons above the tragedy of the situation. Here, it is a question of people who react more "role-consciously" or theatrically in relation to their own role as "happy locals". We have no way of knowing whether they are happy, or what the real reason for the expression is, but the conscious performance gives the local "performers" in the picture, in spite of their dependence on the tourist economy, a kind of symbolic power.

The symbolic power lies in their, by their performance, showing themselves conscious of their stageness and steadfastness in determining relationships. The smiling attitude and the direct reference to the visual setup create an alliance between the photographer/viewer and the local person, which suddenly places the tourist as staged. The photo depicts the tourist as introverted, self-centred – and in the picture, this is objectified from without. That is to say that a certain tourist mode – the ethnocentric tourist gaze in Urry's sense – is portrayed as a partial element of this photo, but it is insufficient to determine how the entire picture can or should be read. The picture objectifies the visiting tourists (who thus take over the inhabitants' place for the ethnocentric gaze); it allots a reciprocity to the inhabitants that competes with the unequivocal balance of power. The viewer of the photo then becomes a meta-tourist, who is no longer part of a culture-clash, but who is a witness to the clash in this photo, which juggles several forms of tourism.

Neither the tourists nor the local people in the picture pose as victims or potential victims, and this acts to give the picture the surplus of meaning that is one of its basic components. The third level of reading the picture is precisely its formal surface level, which is marked by the juxtaposition of elements that cannot be juxtaposed: wreckage, smiles, sunbathers. The picture does not rest in a spontaneous reading, and it is this structural excess that makes the photo dynamic and enigmatic.

The interpretation of this photo shows that the unequivocal balance of power maintained by Urry's perspective can be challenged by a new gaze at the tourist experience as body-invested and body-exposed. So experience-oriented tourism to "black spots" need not necessarily be read as a callous search for an intense, genuine experience, or as ethically problematic because of the ethical imbalance in the relationship between victim and visiting tourist (Urry 1990: 7). The phenomenologically sensing, experiencing body – simply being there, in that place – is an expression of a symbolic exchange with the victims. The "coin" exchanged can be compared to the wordless embrace, the silent empathy.

Authenticity

Who is the Other in Holocaust tourism, which must be regarded as cultural-heritage tourism in the broad sense? Is the Other simply a staged element in my own theatre? (I prove my self-righteousness as a good citizen by visiting this tourist attraction, thus distinguishing myself from the others, who only go to Disneyland to enjoy themselves …) On the contrary, I would say, and especially not when it comes to Eisenmann's experiential work in the centre of Berlin.

I mentioned that Auschwitz as tourist attraction has great authentic value, because its sign-character is indexical. The site has an aura and symbolic wealth in the Benjaminic sense, because it is the actual original crime scene. In his discussion of the originality of a work of art, Benjamin distinguishes between auratic objects and traces. The trace is just that in which the relationship between representation and that which is represented is close (as in the indexical sign), while auratic objects are distinguished by the distance they instil (Bærenholdt & Haldrup 2004). In their article about cultural-heritage tourism for the Viking museum in Roskilde, Bærenholdt and Haldrup find that it is "the replicas, the re-enactments and so forth that enable visitors to 'take possession of things'" (2004: 86). In other words, it is only when cultural heritage has an experiential dimension that it feels authentic. In this connection it is important to distinguish between genuineness and authenticity. Genuineness relates to the object's character of being a genuine trace (hair, shoes, or suitcases that belonged to prisoners in the Auschwitz concentration camp), while authenticity concerns the *bodily-phenomenological* experience of a place, which can involve various types of stage-setting at and of the sites.

When as an analyst one finds that tourists experience stage-set elements of a culture-heritage tourist attraction as more authentic than elements that are "only" traces, the finding refers to precisely the analytic distinction we must make between genuineness and authenticity. Genuineness poses the question of the truth of the trace, while authenticity always concerns the reception of an event, the *experience of authenticity*. The point is that stage-set traces can also make for extremely authentic experiences, just as genuine traces need not have an experiential value.

With the authenticity term, we leave the discussion of the genuineness of traces (truth), and turn to a discussion of the effect of events (pragmatism). The effects can be both pragmatic and affective (like traces on the soul).

Focussing on the bodily-phenomenological experience of something gives rise to specific types of aesthetics. Thus, aesthetics become sense-borne, relational, more open, less elitist than modernistic aesthetics, since it is the relationship between thing/place and the person experiencing it that is in focus (Knudsen & Thomsen 2002: 17). This form of sense-borne and experiential aesthetics developed to a marked degree throughout the art and culture of the 1990s.

Another recurrent aesthetic trait that can be stressed in the expression of the 90's, is the mating of "hot" and "cool" strategies. Beginning with the 90s, a proximity strategy is often mated with "coolness" and distance. In snapshot photography, dogma films, art-performance and installation, and minimalist prose, cool "surface consciousness and affective approach interact" (ibid.: 8). The "hot" strategies can then be designated as those that primarily make an affective approach to the audience, or that have the bodily involvement of the viewer as an element in the shaping of the work or event. The "cool" strategies involve emotional and cognitive distance.

Tom Selwyn introduces a distinction between "cool" and "hot" authenticity that can be used here. Warm authenticity touches on the mythological or meta-narrative character of tourism. In tourism, the relationship between the self and the other is played through as a mythological relationship. The other "derives from belonging to an imagined world which is variously pre-modern, pre-commoditized or part of a benign whole recaptured in the mind of a tourist" (Selwyn 1996: 21). The other is mythologized, but unlike what happens in Orientalism's demonisation and idealisation of the other, this takes place with a social goal in mind: the other stands for a form of sociality that the tourist has lost sight of in his post-modern landscape. Thus the longing for authenticity is still an important driving force for post-modern tourists.

The cool search for authenticity is about the tourist's desire for knowledge. In it, the tourist is viewed as an ethnographer, who in semi-scientific fashion seeks out his object. For Selwyn, cool authenticity is essential, since it is able to dam up tourists' mythological fantasies about the other. If authenticity were not present as a dimension of knowledge, there would be "no way out of an eventual wholesale Disneyfication of one part of the world built on the wasteland of the other" (ibid.: 30).

So we can conclude the discussion of the concept of authenticity as follows: 1) the adjective "authentic" is used about something that is felt and experienced as such, and refers primarily to the reception of places and their staging. It is useful to distinguish between the genuineness of places or phenomena, which has to do with the degree of truth and closeness to the referential, and their authenticity. 2) We then move from a discussion of genuineness and originality on a referential level to a discussion of authenticity on a recipient level. 3) On the recipient level – or more precisely, in the relationship between work/phenomenon and recipient – we can distinguish between "cool" and "hot" effects. The proximity strategy has as a "hot" effect the fact that it inscribes the recipient bodily and affectively, fundamentally creating fellowships. Distance strategies are linked to a dimension of knowledge in the objects and thus create an analytic-reflexive distance.

Holocaust tourism or black-spot tourism in general is, of course, special as regards the discussion of authenticity. As traces, the sites are genuine, and they are all scenes of crimes or located in the metonymic vicinity of the scenes of the actions symbolised. That is to say that these are sites that are sought out because they are traces, so that authenticity is closely linked to genuineness. In Holocaust tourism, all levels behave effectively: the referential truth level, the affective viewer level, and the symbolic re-inscribing level (I come here, but I can leave again).

In the special form of cultural-heritage tourism we find in relation to the Holocaust, the tourist's "other" is the victim. In this form of tourism, a monument over the victims is built, while the viewer does not suffer the same fate. Griselda Pollock sees travelling to and leaving the places again as ethically problematic, and thus maintains the structural reading of the places' representation of the event. "To go, to tour *and to leave*, is to defy that demonic logic, to put 'Auschwitz' back in a place with an entrance *and an exit*, to see its impoverished remains as the closed containers of a history that is past and fading" (Pollock 2005: 176).

My point in this connection is that it is possible to make a form of representation of this gruesome event that is ethically defensible, and that this representational form approaches presentation, i.e. is dependent on the visitor's bodily investment in the phenomenon. Just as in Lehman's photo, the post-Urryan tourist is one who is bodily exposed and bodily invested.

The Memorial to the Murdered Jews of Europe

The Memorial for the Jewish victims of the Holocaust consists of Peter Eisenmann's 19,000 square meters of sculpture park above ground, along with the 800 square meters of information and documentation centre underground. In the centre, the many camps outside Germany are documented, with the stories of victims from each country from which Jews were deported. In addition there is documentation for the high degree to which German Jews were and are an integral part of German history.

The sculpture park consists of 2,700 rectangular stelae, all 95 cm wide and placed at distances of 95 cm. The total length is 2,375 m and the height of the pillars varies from 0 to 4 m. The grid structure is full of holes, which means that new spaces frequently appear inside the structure, either making the passages expand, contract, or occasionally end in a dead end. The informational material on the site states that the memorial explores the relationship between the rational closed system and the chaos and lack of stability that the system nevertheless gives rise to. One might say that there is a great difference in how the memorial is overseen visually, and the experience of moving around in it as an affective space. The floor level constantly varies; rises and falls are incorporated into the structure of the stelae, making the bodily experience slightly dizzying. Rather like the feeling of losing contact with the ground caused by the camera's movement in Lars Von Trier's films.[3]

In the underground documentation centre, we find a great number of stories, texts, knowledge, voices, and pictures. Above ground, in Eisenmann's work, there are no pictures and no texts, merely a room one can enter. And obviously its use varies widely. Some – like children – play, others wander contemplatively about, while others concentrate on attempting to decipher the structure.

On the surface, the memorial maintains the modernistic stricture on images and representation, in that nothing indicates the actual event (no piles of shoes, of hair or possessions). There are no concrete victims present that we as witnesses can recognize as victims. There are no catastrophic scenes. The pictures we carry in our memories of this epoch in European history are certainly present in the imaginations of some of the visitors. But my point with regard to Eisenmann's work is that because of its expanse, it acts as a *place* in the centre of Berlin, a place that because of its aesthetic construction offers the visitor intensity and a special bodily experience. It is a pluralistic place, a memorial, but also an oasis in the city, an intensive space.

It can be advantageous to read the memorial as an emotional geographic place, in which feelings must be understood "experientially and conceptually – in terms of its socio-spatial mediation and articulation rather than as entirely interiorised subjective mental states" (Bondi, Davidson & Smith 2006: 3). We are dealing with an architecture where the intensity arises from the site's position in the metonymical proximity of a "crime scene" to which the visitor's body reacts, and of the experience that the place "calls to" the visitor's bodily investment in it. As previously stated, the symbolic form of exchange at this site is the bodily investment of the visitor.

We recognise bodily investment from certain film genres, but we also know it from the TV-viewer's affective empathy in both collective and individual suffering, confessions, and traumas, in that these events are communicated to us in especially aesthetic manners. In these cases, the viewer has an affective exchange with the screen, and this "politics of pity" (Boltanski 1999) can result in debate, donations of money, or tears. The similarity between the two forms of experience is that the sight of the needy, the traumatised, the outcast, gives rise to a reaction, which can be political, economic or discursive. And this reaction is brought about by the emotions and the bodily experience. In the visual confrontation with suffering, we as viewers are witnesses to others' testimony, and we are eyewitnesses outside the framework of the catastrophic scenarios. To witness the tragedy of others is the same as to recognise the other (Caruth 1995; Laub 1995). To recognise the other via one's own – often physical – reaction, means a re-incorporation in the symbolic order from which the other – because of the catastrophe – has fallen.

In Eisenmann's memorial, the visitor is also a witness, a witness to a traumatic epoch in European history. But where testimony to suffering from all over the world daily intrudes and cannot be avoided because of the media's compression of time and space, the Holocaust Monument is a site one seeks out as a visitor, like any other cultural heritage site. My point here is that with Eisenmann's memorial, we have a *light* physical inscription in the cultural heritage. Here, there is no monument or memorial one visits, reads and circumvents in the ordinary sense. Here, we really have an intensive site, that one enters, and where one has a physical interchange with history. The memorial is an experiential site, and that which is consumed is emotional intensity. In that way, Eisenmann's memorial is an emotional place, child of the increased focus on experiences and physical intensity. The body is not at risk in a form of ritualised overstepping of limits (bungy jump, roller coasters) but the body in this place becomes the coin of exchange with the past.

The memorial is – in spite of its proximity to a crime scene – a thoroughly symbolic place. Emotional ties and fellowships are established between the victims from the past and the survivors of the present through the memorial-visitor's investing body. When Pollock, in his analysis of Auschwitz-Birkenau as current tourist attraction claims that it is ethically offensive as visitor and witness to leave a place from where no one otherwise escaped alive, this reading is linked to Auschwitz-Birkenau as an Erinnerungsort. In that way, Eisenmann's memorial as Denkmal is a thoroughly simulated place with a much freer framework. Auschwitz-Birkenau's genuineness as sign is here replaced by cool authenticity on the level of reception, where the coin of exchange is the body, but where there is an implicit link to a great deal of knowledge. But it does not need to be present in order to experience the place as an intensive emotional geography. One can tell the story to the children who play inside and on top of the memorial.

Summary

My intention in this article has been to propose an alternative to the modernistic structural manner of referring to and representing the Holocaust. The alternative is formulated based on new paradigms in tourist research, and on the reading of Peter Eisenmann's Memorial to the Murdered Jews of Europe as an emotional geography in which the visitor invests his or her body. The question of authenticity is in focus here. In a distinction between cultural-heritage sites as genuine or authentic, Eisenmann's memorial can be designated as authentic because of its physical experiential value. The bodily investment, whose form this article calls cool authentic, is a way of exchanging with and recognising the victims. But it is not the only way: the memorial is also a place where one can be intensively present in the urban space, and in that case, the site offers an aesthetic oasis.

Notes

1 Some people regard Holocaust tourism as part of a larger genre of modern tourism: "black-spot tourism" (Rojek 1997 and Cole 1999), where places like the Bridge over the River Kwai, the highway crossroads between route 466 and 41 near Cholane, California, the place in Dallas (the Texas School Book Depository) where Lee Harvey Oswald shot JFK, the place (the sidewalk outside the Dakota Apartment building) in New York where John Lennon was shot, and the place in the Parisian tunnel where Princess Diana died. However, there is the significant difference between Holocaust tourism and black-spot tourism that black-spot tourism is closely linked to admiration for the dead and cultivation of their stardom. Holocaust tourism cannot be linked to any such cultic worship; it is a journey to a black hole in the history of Europe.
2 The personal, concrete effects as traces, and, of course, the architecture itself, are the focal point of how the Jewish Museum in Berlin represents the event.
3 Especially in *Epidemic and Breaking the Waves*.

References

Barthes, Roland 1983: *Det lyse kammer. Bemærkninger om fotografiet*. Copenhagen: Politisk Revy.
Bondi Liz, Joyce Davidson & Mick Smith (eds.) 2006: Introduction: Geography's 'Emotional Turn'. In: *Emotional Geographies*. Great Britain: MPG Books.
Bærenholdt, Jørgen Ole et al. 2004: *Performing Tourist Places*. Ashgate.
Bærenholdt, Jørgen Ole & Michael Haldrup 2004: On the Track of the Vikings. In: John Urry & Mimi Sheller (eds.), *Tourism Mobilities: Places to Play, Places in Play*, London: Routledge.
Boltanski, Luc 1999[1993]: *Distant Suffering, Morality, Media and Politics*. Cambridge.
Caruth, Cathy 1995: Introduction. In: *Trauma, Explorations in Memory*. Baltimore, London: The Johns Hopkins University Press.
Chouliaraki, Lilie 2003: Moraliseringen af seeren. *Dansk Sociologi*, 14. Årgang, 1. The University of Copenhagen.
Cole, Tim 1999: *Images of the Holocaust. The Myth of the Shoah Business*. Duckworth.
Crouch, David & Nina Lübbren 2003: Introduction. In: *Visual Culture and Tourism*. Oxford, New York: Berg.
Ellis, John 2002: *Seeing Things, Television in the Age of Uncertainty*. London, New York: I.B. Tauris.
Felman, Shoshana & Dori Laub 1992: *Testimony, Crises of Witnessing in Literature, Psychoanalysis, and History*. New York, London: Routledge.
Foster, Hal 1996: *The Return of the Real. The Avant-Garde at the End of the Century*. Cambridge, London: MIT Press.
Friedlander, Saul (ed.) 1992: *Probing the Limits of Representation*. Cambridge, Massachusetts: Harvard University Press.
Jackson, Rhona 2005: Converging Cultures; Converging Gazes; Contextualizing Perspectives. In: David Crouch, Rhona Jackson & Felix Thompson (eds.), *The Media & The Tourist Imagination. Converging Cultures*. London, New York: Routledge.
Knudsen, Britta Timm & Bodil Marie Thomsen 2002: Indledning. In: *Virkelighedshunger – nyrealismen i visuel optik*. Copenhagen: Tiderne Skifter.
Knudsen, Britta Timm 2003 a: Realisme i 50'erne, Visualitet, affekt og traumer i den ny roman. In: *virkelighed, virkelighed! – avantgardens realisme*. Copenhagen: Tiderne Skifter.
Knudsen, Britta Timm 2003 b: The Eyewitness and the Affected Viewer. *Nordicom*, Årgang 24, nummer 2. Göteborg.
LaCapra, Dominick 1998: *History and Memory after Auschwitz*. Ithaca: Cornell.
Laub, Dori 1995: Truth and Testimony: The Process and the Struggle. In: *Trauma, Explorations in Memory*. Baltimore, London: The Johns Hopkins University Press.
Lowenthal, David 1985: *The Past is a Foreign Country*. Cambridge University Press.
Lyotard, Jean-François 1988: *Heidegger et »les juifs«*. Paris: Gallimard.
MacCannell, Dean 1976: *The Tourist, a New Theory of the Leisure Class*. London: Macmillan.
Materials on The Memorial to the Murdered Jews of Europe 2005. Berlin: Nicolai.
Pollock, Griselda 2003: Holocaust Tourism: Being There, Looking Back and the Ethics of Spatial Memory. In: Crouch & Lübbren (eds.), *Visual Culture and Tourism*. Oxford, New York: Berg.
Ricoeur, Paul 2000: *La Mémoire, l'histoire, l'oubli*. Paris: Grasset.
Rojek, Chris 1997: Indexing, Dragging and Social Construction. In: Chris Rojek & John Urry (eds.), *Touring Cultures, Transformations of Travel and Theory*. London, New York: Routledge.
Rosset, Clément 1985: *L'Objet singulier*. Paris: Minuit.
Sandbye, Mette 2001: *Mindesmærker, Tid og erindring i fotografiet*. Copenhagen: Rævens Sorte Bibliotek.
Sartre, Jean-Paul 1940: *L'imaginaire: Psychologie phénoménologique de l'imagination*. Paris: Gallimard.
Selwyn, Tom 1996: Introduction. In: T. Selwyn (ed.), *The Tourist Image. Myths and Myth Making in Tourism*. London: John Wiley and Sons.

Storey, John 2003: *Inventing Popular Culture. From Folklore to Globalization*. Oxford: Blackwell.
Urry, John 1990: *The Tourist Gaze*. London: Sage.
Žižek, Slavoj 2002: *Velkommen til Virkelighedens ørken, Essays om verden efter den 11. September*. Viborg: Informations Forlag.

Britta Timm Knudsen is associate professor, Ph.D., at the Scandinavian Institute, University of Aarhus. Among her recent publications are "It's live. Performativity and Role-playing" in *Performative Realism* by Rune Gade and Anne Jerslev (eds.) 2005 and "Local Cinema: Indexical Realism and Thirdspace in Blue Collar White Christmas by Max Kestner" in *Northern Constellations, New Readings in Nordic Cinema* by Claire Thomson (ed.) 2006. She is currently editing a book (together with Anne Marit Waade): *Investing in Places – Rethinking Authenticity*, forthcoming 2008.

ANNIVERSARIES AND JUBILEES
Changing Celebratory Customs in Modern Times

Ruth-Elisabeth Mohrmann

Every minute, somebody, somewhere is celebrating something. When did customs of celebrating jubilees become a matter of course in festive culture and why and when did we actually start to celebrate them? With the institution of the Holy Year in 1300 an interval of 50 years, later of 25 years, as a celebratory cycle was found which is observed in both secular and Christian celebrations up to the present. Secular jubilees or private anniversaries have a much shorter history. With a few exceptions in early modernity it was not until the nineteenth century that the number of occasions for "celebrating something" started to grow and the differences of celebratory customs broadened.[1]

Keywords: celebratory customs, birthday, jubilee, myth of the decades, self-representation

Do you remember? Let us take a short look back to the year 2005 – Mozart had his two hundred and forty-ninth birthday and Rembrandt van Rijn his three hundred and ninety-ninth – had that been any news for us? Of course it hadn't. But in 2006, the two hundred and fiftieth and four hundredth birthdays of these immortal geniuses were milestones for innumerable events. But we all had our own birthdays, last year as every year – maybe the thirty-ninth or the forty-fourth or even the fiftieth or sixtieth – and every one of us celebrated their own birthday as a personal anniversary in their way.

With the famous w-questions, we can ask who, what, where, when, with whom and how we celebrate and we will quickly find the answers. But one question and one answer is usually left out: why do we celebrate at all?

"The self-evident is the last thing we recognise. It resembles the hare that lies at our very feet" (Jünger 1954: 11).[2] The self-evident nature, with which all the jubilees and anniversaries are celebrated year by year in increasing number, is taken as a given. The laying of the foundation stone of the St. Peter's Basilica in Rome five hundred years ago was remembered in 2006 as well as Friedrich von Schiller's two hundredth day of death, and the four hundredth birthday of the foundation of Giessen University in 2007. But why and since when we automatically follow this compulsive mechanism of celebrating round numbers and the commemoration of more or less important jubilees – this is a question seldom or, in fact, only very recently asked.

In a mixture of a consciousness of tradition and convention, birthdays with a zero (in German they are called round birthdays, "runde Geburtstage") or wedding anniversaries like silver or golden anniversaries are given great attention. That is also the case at work, e.g. twenty-five, forty or fifty years of employment is honoured with gratifications. But particularly commemorations in the public sphere and in the media cannot be thought of without jubilees and anniversaries. Conferences and exhibitions follow the adamant law of the cycles of jubilees as well as communities and businesses – as far away from any sense of historicity they may be. Just consider the jubilee days of the deaths or births of their founders or their founding acts in the pressure of these dates and decide in almost any case: "we got to do something".

Commemoration in certain intervals of time is a popular ritual with a certain automatism. In order to authorize all these memorial acts, it is simply enough to remember the fiftieth, hundredth or even thousandth anniversaries or whatever other attractive number is allocated to commemorating a person or a founding act. This demonstrates awareness of history or at least suggests its existence. Institutions and people are making the most of the dignity of their age, while simultaneously formulating a need for admiring the future by producing jubilees. They propose to be entitled to give the only valid interpretation of the past and to marginalize competing patterns. But the cycles of jubilees have their own history with many transformations due to changing historical contexts. Carrying out jubilees and anniversaries as if it were simply natural often lets us forget the historicity of this fabricated construction of time.

Religious Origins of Jubilee Cycles

Before dealing with the question of historicity of jubilee cycles and anniversaries, it is necessary to investigate their roots. Jubilees date back to the Old Testament. Leviticus 25, 8-55 states that after seven times seven years, i.e. after forty-nine years, a "jobel year" is to follow. *Jobel* is the horn of the ram and the playing of the ram horn was the beginning of this special 50th year. "And you shall hallow the fiftieth year, and proclaim liberty throughout the land to all its inhabitants; it shall be a jubilee for you, when each of you return to his property and each of you return to his family", which means that properties were restored to their original owners and slaves were set free.

The tradition of the jubilee has never really been forgotten during the Middle Ages but the combination of jubilee and the fiftieth year was rather an exception than the rule. The best known exception is the re-burial of Thomas Becket fifty years after his actual death; on this occasion, the archbishop of Canterbury referred directly to the Leviticus text. Much more often jubilees were not fixed to a strictly defined cycle but could be combined with any kind of indulgence: "every time he is forgiven for his sins is a jubilee for the believer". Most important for the modern cycle of jubilees was the combination of the fixed fifty-years-cycle and the non-fixed indulgence cycle – and as it is well-known, this was initiated as the Holy Year in 1300 by Pope Boniface VIII. All the Christians who went on a pilgrimage to Rome in this year and visited the seven (and later on four) main churches received a full indulgence and remission of all sins. Due to the theological interpretation of a double remission of sin and punishment, the Holy Year should not be repeated before one hundred years have passed. But the enormous success of the first Holy Year led to the next one not one hundred years later but as soon as in 1350. After a longer time of experimenting with the interval of thirty-three years – the age of Jesus Christ – in 1468, the rhythm which is valid until today came into existence in 1475. To this day the regular Holy Year takes place every twenty-five years. The general unit for measurement of jubilees was found and until today the cycle of jubilees can be divided by twenty-five as a rule (Chase 1990; Mitterauer 1997; 1998; Müller 2004: 9–14).

The success story of the jubilee cycle is rather long. As the twenty-five-year-cycle of the Holy Year was administered by the papacy, this close tie must be removed to make it available in other contexts. One has to take into account that the decimal system did not gain acceptance until the fifteenth century. And to write in Arabic numbers instead of Roman ones did not become popular any earlier. The triumphal march of the clock (in German we have the bizarre word clockisation, i.e. "Veruhrzeitlichung", for this process) and the slow habituation to think in modern calendar years allowed people to precisely handle time and marked spaces of time. These important changes can only be mentioned here but must be kept in mind.

Protestant and Secular Jubilees

The monopoly of the papacy on the jubilee cycle was a delicate problem in secular and non-Catholic contexts. But the attractiveness of this scaling of time must have been so great that ways had to be found to indulge as well. The earliest references to secular jubilees originate from universities. The German universities in Erfurt and Ingolstadt and the university in Basel, Switzerland, gave a special mention of their 100-year-jubilee of their foundation in 1492, 1572, and 1560, not by jubilee events but by works of art. Four universities in Protestant German territories, Tübingen, Heidelberg, Wittenberg and Leipzig, quickly followed with festive ceremonies of their foundation acts one hundred and two hundred years later. In 1578, 1587, 1602 and 1609 these universities celebrated their own history with speeches, opulent banquets, theatre and music and even members of the court attended the festivities which lasted for several days.

These self-representations on the occasion of the one hundred- and two hundred-years-jubilees were not at all self-evident. It was not long ago that the early Reformation had condemned the Roman Holy Year jubilees as "the Pope's fair". And now the Protestant theology professors argued against "Papist jubilees which only existed for the purpose of superstition and in order to fulfil the Roman addiction to money" and defamed it as a "wholly godless and damned jubilee feast" and as an "outrageous drudgery and seduction". So the arguments for using the same appealing time rhythm had to be different, of course. Vice versa the Protestant theologians underlined the "Christian manner" and the "spirit of Christian revival" in which the university jubilees were celebrated (Müller 2004: 23f).

In fact these university jubilees opened the way and the narrow correlation between the Holy Year and the jubilee cycle was definitely dissolved. In the following decades the jubilee cycle was used for many outstanding occasions, particularly by the Protestant churches – for example, the jubilee of Luther's ninety-five propositions and the beginning of the Reformation in 1617 which was an enormous success. In 1630 the jubilee of the Confessio Augustana followed and in 1655 that of the religious Peace of Augsburg. Catholics harshly criticized particularly the ceremonies of the reformation jubilee in 1617 as "pseudo jubilees". And the Catholic church, in turn, rediscovered the dignity of old age for jubilees – the Millennium of German cloisters such as Reichenau, Amorbach and Oberaltaich in the early eighteenth century were peaks of historical jubilees in the Roman Catholic church (Müller 2004: 15–24).

But as we know – jubilees and anniversaries have not remained in the churches' responsibility, but have become a powerful instrument in the process of "confessionalization". This line will not be pursued further here. Rather, I would like to examine the ways through which the jubilees have made their way from religious to secular realms. A key position was played by the letterpress jubilee of 1640. It was an initiative of five citizens of Leipzig who started a remarkable jubilee festivity for the commemoration of the invention of the letterpress with movable letters two hundred years earlier. They became not only the founders of the tradition of centenary celebrations for this world-changing invention but in a certain sense they have become the founders of another tradition as well. Jubilees have become available for everybody and since then, it was in the responsibility of mankind's creativity and initiative to find new occasions for jubilees (Zwahr 1996; Müller 2004: 32–34). Jubilees could now be arranged by agreement among the members of social groups who were convinced of the relevance of particular events. When dates were not known exactly one could arbitrarily set a date for a new jubilee. Presumably the five printers of Leipzig did not realize what a key role they played in the history of jubilees but since they proposed their scheme, time for jubilees was found again and again.

The Tri-centenary of Freudenstadt: A Bourgeois, Urban Example

It was not until the nineteenth century that the middle classes discovered the fascination of anniversaries and started to create ever new occasions for bourgeois self-representation. Particularly the jubilees of cities and their founding acts have been significant instruments for self-staging their citizens. Although there are some forerunners for early city jubilees around 1700, the summit of these celebratory acts did not start until the middle of the nineteenth century and in Germany particularly after the founding of the Empire in 1871. As an example we will consider the tri-centenary of Freudenstadt in the Black Forest in 1899.

Freudenstadt's case can be seen as a model. It was one of the rather rare cities which really knew the exact date of its foundation. Other cities had to look for other occasions for their jubilees – for the laying of the foundation stone of their churches, for the renovation of historical monuments, for the anniversaries of important historical events or for famous personalities being connected to them by birth or death. The imagination was impressive and the competition between the cities was harsh.

Freudenstadt's three hundred years jubilee combined all important features which have been developed during the nineteenth century. As a rather small and quiet town with less than 6,500 inhabitants, Freudenstadt discovered the possibilities of tourism already in the 1880s and the forthcoming event of the three hundredth anniversary of its ducal foundation in 1899 fit excellently in this scheme. The three-day celebration included everything deemed worthy of representing the town; some of it had already been displayed in numerous other city jubilees in the nineteenth century – the official re-opening of the restored church with a festival service, the opening of a newly erected look-out tower as a special commemoration of the town's founder, ceremonial banquets in the specifically enlarged sports hall, the performance of a play of the town's history and tableaux, a monumental historical procession, fireworks with an Italian night, social gatherings with dance and music, and finally also a children's fête. Even the King of Württemberg and numerous guests of honour visited the celebrations – all presented in a lavishly printed programme. The little town was decorated with gates of honour, flags and arms, garlands and wreaths. And almost all the town people were engaged in the "festive activities which were carried out with great industry and diligence".

Particularly the historical procession is worth looking at in more detail. It was the highlight of the show and attracted a lot of spectators even from afar. A very procession-experienced professor of architecture from Stuttgart was engaged for the organisation. More than 1,200 persons were fitted with costumes specially ordered from Munich; in comparison: in 1890, the much bigger former free city Ulm (36,000 inhabitants) engaged 1,700 participants for its superb historical procession. In Freudenstadt, thirty wagons were splendidly decorated; the necessary work and labour lasted for months. More than two hundred and twenty horses and numerous musical bands were supplied by the military administration – in fact the organisation alone was a huge achievement for such a small town! The historical procession followed the form of others – three parts can be distinguished: the first part was dedicated to concrete occasions of Freudenstadt's history, the second one performed scenes of popular culture such as a wedding procession and showed various groups dressed in regional costumes. The third and last one picked the central themes of agriculture, trade and industry and even tourism. In this last group were mentioned: spa tourists, forest cafés, the Black Forest club, English gentlemen and their butlers, and cyclists. To keep the memory of all these magnificent celebrations alive, commemorative items were sold such as prints of the speeches and new books on Freudenstadt's history (Faix 2001: 11–28).

The Contemporary Explosion of Jubilees

The track record of city jubilees did not end with the nineteenth century. On the contrary, they increased enormously. Nowadays it is not enough to have three-days or one-week celebrations – nowadays the whole year is a never-ending festivity. Preparations start some years in advance by founding organisational committees to stage the most magnificent jubilee ceremonies, new staff in the city's marketing team use all their strength to make the absolute best of it, academic celebrities edit new publications for the occasion not only in one but three, four and more volumes, the possibilities are endless. Everything is tried out; everybody has their own experiences in this field.

For the nineteenth century the city jubilees were said to show the affirmation and the representation of the more and more self-confident bourgeoisie, the strengthening of the "sense of citizenship", often with a patriotic and national tone. The self-confidence in using symbols demonstrating the values and achievements of the bourgeoisie developed more and more. Jubilees and their celebrations are excellent occasions to gain a deeper insight in the manifestation of mentality of societies and their special structure.

Nowadays there really is an explosion of jubilees and not only of cities but of almost everything. We are all part of an "society of adventure" (Schulze 1992), an event society, and it is down to everybody's commitment and inclination to participate or not. But looking at all these jubilees – is it really the particular quantity of time or is the number hundred, thousand and so on only a sign and a signal for essential parts which are not yet known and which are only present in the subconscious? As an example: at the centenary of the service club of Rotary International 2005, what have all the guests really celebrated in thousands over thousands of festivities around the world? An institution, a tradition, or themselves? And why did they organise all these celebrations – due to an obligation, due to pride, or as self-assurance? And why have they done it exactly in this way – with ceremonial banquets in decorated halls, with music and speeches?

To the central question "why" everybody knows an answer, but we hesitate to write it down because it seems too naïve. Everybody does it and has always done it. A lot of things have become so normal and conventional that the established repetition has become obligatory. And historical jubilees possess such a self-evident truth which is generally accepted and therefore seldom questioned. We do not query these acts und in fact it is not necessary. A huge advantage of ritualizing our everyday behaviour is that we are not forced to think about it all the time (Gerndt 1981: 24–26).

Everyday life cannot be thought of without rituals. They express social closeness and the central ceremonies during the year such as Christmas and Easter – to take the Christian examples – or during the life cycle such as birthdays, name days, weddings or professional anniversaries – all give everyday life its specific structure. To celebrate all these events will not be familiar for everyone. But there is one field of anniversaries where one cannot escape – it is the field of our own private anniversaries. It is worth to have a look at the history of this tradition.

Private Anniversaries

Concerning the tradition of celebrating the anniversaries of our personal birthdays, the story is even shorter than that of the jubilee. Of course one may look back at the ancient world and find the interesting fact of a commemoration of one's own birthday in every month every time the date of the day returned.

But the tradition of our modern celebratory customs of personal birthdays dates back to the Middle Ages. The necessary requirement was to know the date of one's own birth and this information was only extant for the nobility and the high clergy. First references for birthday celebrations of European high nobles cannot be found before the twelfth century even when considering the data revealed by medieval literature. It was not until the seventeenth century that the bourgeoisie accepted the celebration of birthdays. And rural societies did not practice birthday celebrations before the nineteenth and – as we will see – in many cases not until the twentieth century. In the countryside, church registers sometimes did not record the date of birth, and this was the case until the middle of the eighteenth century. Early modern records of testimonies are full of references that witnesses did not know either their age or their birthday. Another interesting aspect is the etymological origin of the German word "Geburtstag" for birthday. The middle high German *geburt-tac* (old high German *giburtitago*) was only the day of birth but not the anniversary of it. It was Martin Luther who translated 'dies natalis' as 'birthday' but considerable time passed before 'birthday' as an anniversary became a customary expression.

Birthdays and Name Days

But why did it take so long until rural societies – and they did not stand alone – took to the custom of celebrating birthdays? Did they not have anniversaries to celebrate? Of course they did, but we have to further investigate one aspect which we have neglected so far – the distinction between the confessions. What we have to take into account is the development of different scenarios – on the one hand the Catholic name days or Saint's days, on the other hand the Protestant birthdays. Reformation and Counter-Reformation have changed the context for the developments in Catholic and Protestant countries and regions profoundly. The Council of Trent and particularly the Catechismus Romanus of 1566 interrupted the tradition of birthday festivities which the European high nobility had already celebrated since the Middle Ages. The Calendar of Saints became the authority for all Catholic believers, transcending individual birthdays. Exclusively the names of Saints could be used for baptising children. Protestants, with the abolition of the veneration of the saints, however, were missing the Calendar of Saints and its large inventory of names. New Christian names were created such as Gotthilf, Fürchtegott or Leberecht – names without a name day tradition but still with a reference to religion (the equivalent in the English language would be virtuous names like Faith, Hope, Chastity etc.). But in the long run, this lack of canonised names and new creations permanently supported the turn toward the individual birthday and its memory. Even though the celebration of birthdays is the older tradition, these anniversaries stand for modernity. Name days were linked to the cyclical time whereas birthdays stood for the linear time and for individualisation.

Let us have a look at these different landscapes in the first half of the twentieth century. The strict division: here Catholic name days, there Protestant birthdays had already lost its distinct border when Catholics started celebrating their birthdays toward the end of the nineteenth century. Higher social levels celebrated them earlier, as did the urban population in contrast to the rural. Around 1930 we can find the following pattern:

Only birthday – Protestant
Birthday and name day – Catholic cities, industrial/urban places and mixed confessional regions
Only name day – Catholic villages and small Catholic towns

Regions where only name days were celebrated have become very rare but even in the 1970s they had not totally disappeared (Böhm 1938; Dürig 1954; Zender 1977: 168; Hopf-Droste 1979; Bausinger 1994). And – as I can add as an inhabitant of a mostly Catholic rural region in Westphalia – up to the present the name day is the most important anniversary for devout Catholics, the occasion that calls for a formal celebration in a large circle of family and relatives. Only for the relatively informal birthday festivity, Protestant neighbours are invited, too.

There are – as another example – similar results to be found in Finland in the 1940s. The dissemination of name days which was accepted from Sweden since the eighteenth century had not yet spread throughout the whole country when it was overwhelmed by the birthday. Particularly since the 1940s the celebration of the so-called important birthdays (fiftieth, sixtieth, sixty-fifth, seventieth, seventy-fifth etc.) spread through the whole of Finland (Talve 1966: 46). Looking back to Central Europe we can add that the increase of birthday celebrations in Catholic regions started with the anniversaries. But one has to emphasize that these notable birthdays did not gain a foothold before the end of the First World War. Birthday parties for children had become popular not much earlier either. In the nineteenth century only the children of nobles and of urban-bourgeois groups have celebrated their birthdays, although not regularly (Falkenberg 1984: 16-27).

To count the years of one's life is presently an integral element of our habitual way of thinking. But it is also an aspect of the modern process of quantification. Highly important birthdays as the Nativity and the Nativity of Mary have nothing to do with counting days, months, years or centuries. They are integrated in the church year and their dates were fixed in a rather long process. In a certain sense this tradition still exists. The "Emperor's birthday" in the Habsburg and Wilhelminian time had been the event itself and not the emperor's actual sixty-second or whichever birthday. And nowadays the Dutch "Koniginnendag" and the birthday of the English Queen are even celebrated on the "wrong" day (Hopf-Droste 1979: 236).

We know with C.P. Snow (1961: 383) that nine out of ten traditions have their origins in the second half of the nineteenth century. Looking back at the jubilee cycle, this assumption seems correct. But we can also observe notable changes in the celebratory customs in the twentieth century. And we know about the remarkable phenomenon of "invented traditions" with their astonishing careers, even when they are only regional (Hobsbawm & Ranger 2004). An example: Amongst their frolicking peers, some unmarried German bachelors are forced to sweep the stairs of the town hall or the church which was soiled with waste, paper or rice by their friends on their thirtieth birthday. A large audience of spectators is waiting for the moment of deliverance by the kiss of a virgin. The whole spectacle is crude, full of sexual allusion and fuelled with large quantities of alcohol. But in North West Germany it has become very popular in the last decades with a set of essential parts such as announcements in the newspapers with photos and clumsy rhymes, special costumes, music and specific methods to lengthen the procedure. In fact it is a humiliating reprimand (*Rügebrauch*) which has already been copied with the thirtieth birthday of unmarried women (they have to clean door handles – *Klinken putzen*) and the twenty-fifth birthday of both sexes when still unmarried. None of these customs is of old age and even in the city of Bremen which is said to be the place of origin for the sweeping of the steps in the 1950s these are customs of middle class and rural groups today (Simon 1998; Ehlert 2005).

Of course there are much more private jubilees than personal birthdays or name days. To celebrate one's wedding anniversaries seems to be an invention of the bourgeoisie as well. Particularly the celebration of silver (twenty-five) or golden (fifty) weddings were already named such in the eighteenth century but seemed to have peaked since the second half of the nineteenth century. In the nineteenth century they illustrated very convincingly the bourgeois ideals of the family home, conjugal love and faithfulness. The Dutch are again ahead of the other European nations – a Dutch medallion minted for a golden wedding anniversary is already known from the 1620s and shows the images which have become popular later: the family arms and two intertwined hands (Müller 2004: 43).

Personal anniversaries are somehow awkward events for the individual concerned. Celebrating one's seventieth, eightieth birthday, one's golden confirmation or golden wedding are not only happy occasions – they are always a *memento mori* as well. This is an important difference to the jubilees of transpersonal systems as states, institutions, enterprises etc. – these gain more and more dignity and value (sometimes economic value) by age and especially by old age. Tradition sells.

Jubilees in the Professional Life

The structure of individual biographies shows significant other aspects as well. Employees are nowadays celebrated for their many years of service in enterprises small or large. At first glance, this seems to be inherited from the industrialisation and its work force. The number of gratifications, of jubilee certificates, of "Treuezeichen" (special gifts for long-standing loyalty) has increased enormously since the second half of the nineteenth century. The enterprises started at the same time with a special kind of jubilee which became the centre of special factory feasts. The production of the five hundredth or the thousandth or the three thousandth railway engine has been highly celebrated as well as the production of the five thousandth rotary printing press or the ten thousandth floodlight – all these jubilee products from Esslingen to Berlin, from Munich to Nuremberg have been accompanied by festivities with special honours for long-standing employees. Until now, these individual jubilees and gratifications are in a certain sense "voluntary employers' contribution". The aspect of loyalty marks a specific rite de passage in the factory festivities with a fixed set of ceremonies. The variety of gifts for the employees is large and characterized by the spirit of the times but there are some indispensable "evergreens" like golden watches, medallions and a certificate from the enterprise. Colleagues were freer in their choice of gifts as the entrepreneurs were, but for decades armchairs – later TV-armchairs – have been winners (Köhle-Hezinger 1993; 2004; 2005).

But there are origins for jubilees in professional life which go much farther back in time. Priests and professors have been the first for whom we have come to know of their celebration of their fiftieth year of inauguration. Both churches celebrated theses jubilees and surprisingly enough it was a Protestant superintendent for whom it was first and exceptionally early recorded, in Leipzig 1568. That does not mean at all that the Protestants have more and more given up their dissociation from the "popish" Holy Year and its fifty-years-cycle. In the first half of the eighteenth century, the "Historical Encyclopedia of Protestant Jubilant Priests" (Groß 1727–1746) was published in three large volumes. In the working world of university professors those who were able to celebrate their fifty-years-jubilee of starting their university career are said to be a very rare species. But the fifty-years-jubilee of the doctoral degree ceremony is an often solemnly celebrated festivity until today, originating from the late seventeenth century. And with the phrase of the "fifty-year old man" Immanuel Kant did not mean Kant at his fiftieth birthday but at the fiftieth anniversary of his doctorate. As far as we know, the professors of universities and of famous schools have been the forerunners for secular professional jubilees. Civil servants in large cities – i.e. Vienna and Dresden – are the next example in the late eighteenth century. From the beginning of the nineteenth century a twenty-five-year-cycle came into existence for personal professional jubilees (Müller 2004: 47–49).

Thinking and Counting in Decades and Centuries

Only one peculiar tradition of images should be mentioned here. The self-evidence of contemporary thinking and counting in decades was unknown to the Middle Ages. The change from the cyclical train of thought to the linear one can be well followed in the pictures of the medieval wheel of life to the early modern staircase of life. The medieval idea of the wheel of life was influenced by the wheel of Fortune which pulls the men up but throws them down again. The fifteenth century still knew pictures of the wheel of life but pictures of seven or ten ages side by side became more and more popular. Since the early sixteenth century the first pictures of the staircases of ages emerged. Since then this special picture has had an extraordinary career until today and it still is a vivid sign for thinking in decades, emphasizing the importance of the transitory phase, i.e. the step into the next decade (*Lebenstreppe* 1983; Bringéus 1988).

The victory of the decimal system was a very long process. Let us have a short look at the turn of the centuries. Due to the spokespersons of the learned elite of the nineteenth century it was well known in all European countries that the turn of the century could not be celebrated before the end of 1900. Curiously enough in Germany, most of the festivities took place already at the beginning of 1900 due to the order of Emperor William II who even made a delicate slip in ordering the celebration for "1 January 1899" (Brendecke 1999: 226). Bavaria, Saxonia and Württemberg ignored this wrong call in Prussia and critical newspapers wrote about a "commanded premature birth of the century" (ibid.: 238). Due to the spokesperson of the not so learned media the twentieth century was only ninety-nine years long and very little resistance was recorded. The magic of the zeros was overpowering. But it is known for the little town Staffelstein in Franconia not to have celebrated the turn of the century before the end of 2000 – Staffelstein is the birthplace of the mathematical genius Adam Riese (Köstlin 2002: 11).

The decision for the fixed date of the turn of the century in 1900 was made very late (December 1899!) whereas the organisation of the last millennium ceremonies started more than a decade in advance – such a digit change asked for the most splendid festivities! Jubilees and anniversaries are nowadays creating huge numbers of workplaces and are considered important economic factors. With Aleida Assmann we may attribute three functions to the anniversaries: interaction and participation, self-representation (*Wir-Inszenierungen*) and impulses for reflection (Assmann 2005: 310f; Binder 2001).

Conclusion
The victory of the decimal-classification is a victory of popular culture as well. Bringing the decimals into the world of myths is a victory of the popularity of the zeros, of the aesthetics of the clean-cut decade and thus decimals have become cult figures. The scaling of our memory and the myth of the decades as well as the staircase of ages are in a certain sense a plausible invention to reduce complexity. Since Eric Hobsbawm's "Invention of Traditions" has become a commonplace even in early morning TV-entertainment, all the revitalized symbols are said to be fakes. Here it is worth to look back a little deeper in history. It was the Renaissance "ars inveniendi" which already asked for bourgeois education and literacy to decode mythological quotations from ancient records. As we know it from baroque festivities with all their grand parades and unexpected sequences of images it was important to recognise quotations as such and to decipher the new sense behind them.

Classical scales of cyclical conception of history have divided epochs in phases of beginning, building and arrival or crisis, or have offered a morphological periodicity of birth – blooming – ripeness and death. Modern scales are working with absolute chronology, with centuries and short time units which clearly show how strong our thought is determined by these scales. "The long eighteenth century" in English history lasts from 1688 to 1820 or 1832, "the long nineteenth century" lasts from 1789 until 1914 or 1917, the twentieth century, accordingly, is a short one from 1918 to 1991 (first by Eric Hobsbawm). The Germanized ethnocentric perspective has the twentieth century ending in 1989 (Köstlin 2002).

Decades are not a natural category but rather invented and accustomed to by our habit of thinking and decimal scaling. In analogy today's celebratory customs of anniversaries have established a practice where even supermarkets and retail shops celebrate the fifth and tenth jubilee as outstanding events. The sense of these time units must not be verified, they are completely arbitrary. Jubilees and anniversaries are omnipresent. They belong to the progress of life and play a key role in structuring time through fixed stations and marks – in private and family life, in work life such as for institutions, social groups and states. Jubilees and anniversaries are challenging – but only in the common frame of the known celebratory customs. Heads of protocol, members of advisory boards just as colleagues, friends and family members must decide to accept the traditional signs and rituals without questions, to create new ones – or to capitulate.

Notes
1 An earlier draft of this paper was presented as a NIAS Seminar lecture on March 9, 2006 at the Netherlands Institute of Advanced Studies (NIAS) for Humanities and Social Sciences, Wassenaar. I am deeply indebted to NIAS, to their entire staff and to all other fellows for the the splendid research opportunities and a wonderful time in Wassenaar.
2 All translations of originally German quotes are my own.

References
Assmann, Aleida 2005: Jahrestage – Denkmäler in der Zeit. In: Paul Münch (ed.), *Jubiläum, Jubiläum … Zur Geschichte öffentlicher und privater Erinnerung*, pp. 305–314. Essen: Klartext Verlag.
Bausinger, Hermann 1994: *Happy Birthday! Zur Geschichte des Geburtstagsfestes*. Tübingen: TVT Medienverlag.
Binder, Beate 2001: Jahrestag. In: Nicolas Pethes & Jens Ruchatz (eds.), *Gedächtnis und Erinnerung. Ein interdisziplinäres Lexikon*, pp. 290–291. Reinbek: Rowohlt.
Böhm, Fritz 1938: *Geburtstag und Namenstag im deutschen Volksbrauch*. Berlin, Leipzig: De Gruyter.
Brendecke, Arndt 1999: *Die Jahrhundertwenden. Eine Geschichte ihrer Wahrnehmung und Wirkung*. Frankfurt, New York: Campus Verlag.
Bringéus, Nils-Arvid 1988: Pictures of the Life Cycle. *Ethnologia Scandinavica* 18: 5–33.
Chase, Malcolm 1990: From Millennium to Anniversary: The Concept of Jubilee in Late Eighteenth- and Nineteenth-Century England. *Past and Present* 129 (1990): 133–147.
Dürig, Walter 1954: *Geburtstag und Namenstag. Eine liturgiegeschichtliche Studie*. München: Zink Verlag.
Ehlert, Kerstin 2005: *Dreißig – ledig – lustig? Moderne Bräuche am 30. Geburtstag*. Göttingen: Schmerse Verlag.

Faix, Gerhard 2001: Städtische Erinnerungskultur im Königreich Württemberg. *Die alte Stadt. Zeitschrift für Stadtgeschichte, Stadtsoziologie und Denkmalpflege* 28 (2001): 11–28.

Falkenberg, Regine 1984: *Kindergeburtstag. Ein Brauch wird ausgestellt*. Berlin: Staatliche Museen Preussischer Kulturbesitz.

Gerndt, Helge 1981: Europäische Ethnologie – und was ein Schuljubiläum damit zu tun hat. 17-28. In Helge Gerndt, *Kultur als Forschungsfeld. Über volkskundliches Denken und Arbeiten*. München: Beck Verlag.

Groß, J.M. 1727–1746: *Historisches Lexicon Evangelischer Jubel-Priester*. 3 vols. Nürnberg, Schwabach.

Hobsbawm, Eric & Terence Ranger (eds.) 2004 (first edition 1983): *The Invention of Tradition*. Cambridge: Cambridge University Press.

Hopf-Droste, Marie-Luise 1979: Der Geburtstag. Ein Beitrag zur Entstehung eines modernen Festes. *Zeitschrift für Volkskunde* 75 (1979): 229–237.

Jünger, Ernst 1954: *Das Sanduhrbuch*. Frankfurt a.M.: Klostermann.

Köhle-Hezinger, Christel 1993: Treuezeichen. Zur kulturellen Kodierung industrieller Identifikation und Gratifikation. In: Michael Dauskardt & Helge Gerndt (eds.), *Der industrialisierte Mensch*, pp. 233–251. Hagen: Westfälisches Freilichtmuseum.

Köhle-Hezinger, Christel 2004: Zeit – Ritual – Fest: Jubilarkultur im Industriezeitalter. In: Winfried Müller (ed.), *Das historische Jubiläum. Genese, Ordnungsleistung und Inszenierungsgeschichte eines institutionellen Mechanismus*, pp. 291–308. Münster: Lit Verlag.

Köhle-Hezinger, Christel 2005: Dinge, Orte, Zeiten: Private Jubiläen. In: Paul Münch (ed.), *Jubiläum, Jubiläum … Zur Geschichte öffentlicher und privater Erinnerung*, pp. 209–220. Essen: Klartext-Verlag.

Köstlin, Konrad 2002: 'Wenden' und Skalen. Zäsuren als Ordnung unserer Erinnerung. In: Konrad Köstlin, Peter Niedermüller & Herbert Nikitsch (eds.), *Die Wende als Wende? Orientierungen Europäischer Ethnologien nach 1989*, pp. 9–26. Wien: Verlag des Instituts für Europäische Ethnologie.

Die Lebenstreppe. Bilder der menschlichen Lebensalter 1983. Köln: Rheinland-Verlag.

Mitterauer, Michael 1997: Anniversarium und Jubiläum. Zur Entstehung und Entwicklung öffentlicher Gedenktage. In: Emil Brix & Hannes Stekl (eds.), *Der Kampf um das Gedächtnis. Öffentliche Gedenktage in Mitteleuropa*, pp. 23–89. Wien, Köln, Weimar: Böhlau Verlag.

Mitterauer, Michael 1998: *Millennien und andere Jubeljahre – Warum feiern wir Geschichte?* Wien: Picus Verlag.

Müller, Winfried 2004: Das historische Jubiläum. Zur Geschichtlichkeit einer Zeitkonstruktion. In: Winfried Müller (ed.), *Das historische Jubiläum. Genese, Ordnungsleistung und Inszenierungsgeschichte eines institutionellen Mechanismus*, pp. 1–75. Münster: Lit Verlag.

Schulze, Gerhard 1992: *Die Erlebnisgesellschaft: Kultursoziologie der Gegenwart*. Frankfurt am Main: Campus Verlag.

Simon, Michael 1998: Moderne Brauchinnovation. Geschichte und Funktion des Treppenfegens beim 30. Geburtstag. *Jahrbuch für Volkskunde NF* 21 (1998): 157–177.

Snow, C.P. 1961: *The Masters*. London: MacMillan.

Talve, Ilmar 1966: *Namens- und Geburtstagstraditionen in Finnland*. Helsinki: Suomalainen Tiedeakat.

Telesko, Werner 1996: Die Wiener historischen Festzüge von 1879 und 1908. Zum Problem der dynastischen Identitätsfindung des Hauses Österreich. *Wiener Geschichtsblätter* 51 (1996): 133–146.

Zender, Matthias 1977: Glaube und Brauch. Fest und Spiel. In: Günter Wiegelmann, Matthias Zender, Gerhard Heilfurth (eds.), *Volkskunde. Eine Einführung*, pp. 132–197. Berlin: Erich Schmidt Verlag.

Zwahr, Hartmut 1996: Inszenierte Lebenswelt: Jahrhundertfeiern zum Gedenken an die Erfindung der Buchdruckerkunst. Buchgewerbe, Buchhandel und Wissenschaft. *Geschichte und Gesellschaft* 22 (1996): 5–18.

Ruth-Elisabeth Mohrmann, Ph.D., is Professor of European Ethnology at Münster University. Recent research and publications include conflict and rituals in the visual culture of Early Modern Europe, auctions and second-hand goods, as well as material culture, and urban history.
(ruth.mohrmann@uni-muenster.de)

THE MEANING OF WEAVING
Textiles in a Museum Magazine

Anneli Palmsköld

What does it mean to study textile objects? Is it possible to use the textiles themselves to illuminate issues of production, use and interpretation? This is the main questions discussed in the article, taking a category of interior textiles from the eighteenth and nineteenth centuries in museum collections as a starting point. By using phenomenology as a method the researchers' experiences of the studied objects are seen as a way of understanding the textiles to be able to contextualize them in time and place. When studying the textiles the process of weaving, the creation of the patterns and the design of the fabric that follows by the use of them, are some of the aspects to analyze. What do things communicate and how is it possible to understand the message?

Keywords: materiality, textiles, museums, weaving, home decorating

Inside the Storage Room

Brown cardboard boxes in different sizes wait on shelves beside rolls of material covered with silk paper or cotton fabric. Unwrapping the packages, one is overwhelmed by beautiful textiles, made of exquisite materials and decorated with wonderful patterns in many different colours. From the inside of the anonymous boxes and rolls – a whole world of colour and design rises towards you! The textiles are to be handled with care, for they represent important skilfulness in the eighteenth and nineteenth centuries, often representative objects made by women.

The procedure of unwrapping these packages takes place in a museum storage room. That is where most of the textiles are to be found, not as parts of exhibitions but as parts of the enormous collections of objects in museums. At the end of the nineteenth century when the contemporary map of Swedish museums was drawn, textiles were important objects to collect.[1] They were considered to be unique as they represented a historic way of producing and reproducing textiles. One has to remember that industrialization started with mechanising the production of textiles. The products delivered from modern factories were just the opposite of these handmade textiles, collected as representations of the pre-modern world. While modern textiles were made by machines, many in succession and thereby seen as artificial, the old ones were made by hand and considered to be authentic or unique. When discussing art, some theorists argued that the mother of all art was textile art (Semper 1860). To study and to collect pre-modern textiles was, according to them, to take part in constructing art history or the evolution of art. Since fashions and home decorating textiles were the first material areas to be changed as a consequence of industrialization, older homely things were a top priority when collecting for museums. Visiting a museum meant finding other contrasting homes decorated with domestic objects, especially when exhibited in constructed interiors as Artur Hazelius did in his "Scandinavian-Ethnographic Collection" and Skansen.

The older textiles were once hot stuff for the museum pioneers – as representations and evidence of cultural evolution, as art artefacts or as significant objects for comparing homes and fashion. Encountering textiles in a museum context means something quite different today. From a status as key symbols, they have transformed into rather dead material, considered hard to use for public purposes or research. Since the documentation of them is brief, it seems difficult to contextualize them, for example to discuss who actually made them, how they were used and what people thought about them. But is the lack of documentation only to be seen as a barrier to learning about them? What about using the objects themselves as an empirical base for research?

In this article I will discuss a certain category of textiles – interior textiles from the eighteenth and nineteenth centuries – in terms of their materiality.[2] The underlying question is whether it is possible to use the textiles themselves to illuminate issues of production, use and interpretation. At the same time I also focus on methodological concerns for using textiles as a primary source when asking this question: What does it mean to study textile objects?

Starting the Research Project

Most of the textiles in focus have been collected between 1886, when Halland's Museum Association was founded, and the 1930s, when the great period of collecting objects for museums declined.[3] The textiles were gathered in the museum collections in different ways. Some of them were gifts, some were given to the museum through testaments and some were bought from individuals, auctions or antique dealers. Searching for good and interesting things to collect went on alongside the receipt of gifts and receiving offers to buy. During the late nineteenth century folk textiles and other objects considered as folk art turned from primary use in farm households to commodities in a new context of urban life, bourgeois ideology and modernity.[4] The museums took part in this business as one of the agents involved in the market.

After being collected, the objects were numbered, measured and described in the museum catalogue. The descriptions are vague, and basing inquiry on them, the researcher cannot separate one textile from another unless they were photographed to be identified. The descriptions can be characterized as visual as they express in words what the eyes can see and the hands can feel. Techniques and materials are often described but patterns are seldom transformed into words. Relevant information about the textiles and about the human subjects creating and using them is missing. Too often the provenance is not known. It seems to me as if it has not been noticed when they were collected. One reason is that the objects were considered as collective representations or specific types in a material categorization based on form criteria.[5] Inscribed in this kind of interpretation, the individuals behind each object are of little interest.

It is often said that the museum catalogues are prepared and created to be sources for research. Since the information is brief, it is very difficult to analyze the catalogue as a text to be read separately from the object. Instead, one has to analyze the text and the objects together as one unit. It is when interfacing textual and material sources that the most interesting discussions can be made. The catalogue alone, though, can be used for legal and administrative purposes as proof of ownership and evidence for valuing the collections in order to insure them.

I have used the catalogue as a written structure representing the collection and as a starting point before studying the actual textile objects. With the help of the catalogue I have estimated the volume of the items, and, at best, I have been able to find out what kinds of textiles the collection contains. When using the catalogue, though, it was important to read the information from a critical point of view. The terminology is for example often inadequate, leading to misunderstandings. The notes on the provenance, the creator or the user that are missing make it difficult to frame and contextualize these actual objects.

The lack of information in the catalogue led me to study the things themselves in order to analyze them on the basis of the questions concerning production and use. When planning the research project I had hoped to find information about the producers and the users of the textiles. My intent was to find the individuals behind the objects, the creators whose important work I was very much impressed by. But unfortunately I could hardly find any information of this kind in the catalogue. When my research project became locally known, I was contacted by private collectors and by persons who had inherited interior textiles from relatives. They wanted to know more about their textiles and offered to let me study them. When interviewing the owners, I soon found out that they also hardly knew anything about the context of the textiles. At times someone knew the provenance, but no one could with certainty give me the name of the producer or the user. The owners were very uncertain about the individuals behind the objects. The reason, as I found it, was that no one had used the textiles for a very long time. The narratives in which they once were inscribed had been forgotten.

My conclusion was to concentrate on the actual objects for the research – the interior textiles as they appear in the museum collection. I was curious about what it would mean to use the textiles as a source for research alongside the more traditional textual sources. What can one learn from things, information that cannot be found elsewhere? And is it possible to reread "dead" material to bring it back to life again?

To Study Textile Objects

Studying textile objects as they appear in museum collections means basically going to the magazine where they are kept in order to bring them out to an examination room. The textiles are put on a large table to be unpacked from the protective covering. The table just outside the magazine is also the place where one can roll out or unfold the textiles to come really close to them. Since the study room and the table are quite small, one can bring forward only a few textiles at the same time. Some cover the whole table, so you have to go around it many times to be able to inspect and to experience the fabric in detail. Some of them are long enough to cross the table several times when rolled out. Noting my observations on paper, I start with questions concerning the name of each textile, technique(s), material(s), creative concerns, form, patterns, usage, secondary usage, tracks of wear and damage. I also select the fabrics or details to photograph and note why a picture is important in each case.

The phenomenological method of approaching the studied objects is an inspiration. Phenomenology frames the human being as sensory, experiencing and interpreting the world through her senses and through her body. From an individual point of view, "being-in-the-world" means experiencing the world by feeling, smelling, seeing, listening and tasting and not only intellectually by reflecting on it. Studying textile objects in a phenomenological way is to use one's own senses and to transform one's experiences into words when describing them. The simple question is a good starting point. What do I see? How does the fabric feel in my hands? How is it made? Why is it created in this particular way? To go to the things themselves asking this kind of simple questions is to come closer to each actual textile as well as the people who created and used it. This does not mean the researchers' experiences are the same as those of the creators and users long ago. This kind of experiencing through the senses is just as culturally embedded as other expressions of human activities. The method is rather one among others towards finding a way of understanding the textiles to be able to contextualize them.

Inspired by the German philosopher Hannah Arendt, I find the textile objects as results of what she called "work," meaning the human activity which takes tangible forms, such as material objects (Arendt 1998). The textiles materialize practice, individual producers and their creative aims. Pointing out the connection between the textile objects and the conditions of creation means concentrating on these questions: How was each fabric made? What choices did the creator make while producing a peace of fabric? What was more important or less important in the process? What does the actual textile tell us?

Transforming Experiences and Observations into Words

Most of our sensory-based impressions we keep in silence. As human beings we are capable of feeling, but we do not express every feeling in words. Sometimes we do not need to, and sometimes it is difficult to find words that express what we feel. But not only impressions and experiences can go unverbalized; even practice itself and learning practical skills are processes with few words and more learning by doing. A skilled person uses the body and the senses when judging the moments of production. To sense failure is a bodily feeling of things going wrong. Correcting means to undo or redo some moments in the process of creation. The weaving of the textiles was an individual process, a matter for the woman who sat alone by the loom controlling the creation of each fabric. When teaching young girls to be skilled weavers, of course she had to use words to explain what she did and why. Verbalizing every moment in the process, though, can never be a substitute for the knowledge of skill situated in the body. While learning how to weave, or any other skilled labour, one has to acquire this "tacit knowledge" that leads the person to do good work and to develop her skill. Starting with simple techniques and patterns, the work gets more and more challenging as the skill improves.

One of the problems when using the phenomenological method concerns how to transform the subjective experiencing of the objects into words. When reading the notes from studying the textiles, I soon found out the difficulties in expressing my own impressions. From a methodological point of view I was interested in answering the simple questions in a simple way, not yet to analyze but instead to describe, in order to use the descriptions later as the basis of analyzing contextual matters. Comparing the notes made me aware of how inadequate words can be. Without remembering which textile object every note referred to, it was difficult to tell the differences among them, though the objects actually do differ from each other. The solution to this problem was trying to note differences as well as similarities among the textiles in order to be able to identify each one of them. Another solution was trying harder to find words, to be able to describe more precisely the meeting with the objects. In short I tried hard to improve the descriptions. The third way was to use photographs for remembering. This struggling over words and the use of the language has made me reflect on the possibilities of communication, and I have come to think of the textile objects as embodying a language of their own – or of their creators.

The Language of Practice

An underlying structure in contemporary Western society is the necessity of knowing how to read and write. Communication, transactions and relationships are based on a textual ground, and writing and reading belong to everyday life for most people. When the textiles of my research were produced and used, the practical skills of the creators and users were just as necessary when coping with everyday life. Not being able to work using the body or practical skills was a real problem for individuals as well as for every household responsible for keeping the members. Even small children, handicapped men and women and elderly people had to contribute to the household work to the best of their ability. When it comes to textiles, a four-year-old boy or girl could be helpful in the process of preparing the linen or wool before weaving. During the weaving process they prepared the spools for the weaver in order to make the work proceed without interruption. When growing older they participated in more and more complex practical tasks that developed their skill.

This familiarity with practical matters must have left its mark not only in practice but also in minds and in relations. The spoken and the written words are then replaced by the language of practice and of skill, materialized in objects made by hand. To study objects, then, is to study the creator and the creative process.

When studying the past one often asks the question of how to represent the speechless people, those who cannot be found in archives and those who are not represented in words. The textual tracks left to us to read, represent a domination of men of age, since they, from a legal point of view, were seen as masters of the household whereas women were considered to be incapable of managing their affairs (except for widows). But in a time and culture structured by practice, the tracks to look for are not at first textual. Rather, they are to be found in the results of practice – in the objects. Producing textiles, in the sense of weaving, was a female form of household production made for the family's use or for selling.[6] Woven textiles are to be seen as tracks from the women of the past, and when analyzing them we can say something about the conditions of the creator – the woman.

The French philosopher Paul Ricoeur defines texts as discourses established in words (Ricouer 1988: 33). When reading this definition I was inspired to think of the textiles as discourses established in material objects. To analyze the textile objects, then, is, according to Ricouer's definition, an attempt to discuss the conditions and the context where every textile was produced and used. The question is, in which discourses were they inscribed?

In the following I will point out some examples of the results of my research, putting focus on what production of knowledge a close study of textiles can bring forth. The analysis is based on the observation notes written down when studying each fabric. The discussion concentrate on the issues of the process of weaving, the materials used and how the colours varied.

The Process of Weaving

The interior textiles are made of white linen[7] as a ground weave with patterns of linen (blue), linen (blue) and cotton (red) mixed, cotton (red) or wool (dark blue). In the weaving process the weaver started by using the white linen in order to enter the work. The first white part (the ground weave), made in a technique called tabby, was followed by thoroughly planned sequences of patterns in weft-pattern tabby, type "opphämta". While weaving a long piece of fabric of at least seven or eight meters, the weaver made five or six patterns in a row with white parts in between, followed by the most beautiful and difficult pattern for the centre part, and finally repeating the sequences once again in the opposite order. The popular expression for ordering patterns like this from a centre point is to "reflect" them. To be able to reflect the patterns one has to remember each detail of them and in which order to weave them. It seems as if weavers knew how to weave a pattern without relying on instructions about the patterns or on woven textiles as prototypes. The skill of a weaver apparently implied a capacity to remember patterns through knowing how to weave them by doing them.

The patterns and the sequences are designed to be equilateral in order to be able to weave them in both directions towards and from the centre of the textile. The skilled weaver had to image the result to be able to plan the work. This was necessary not only in order to place the patterns in the right row and to know how to weave them, but also to plan the consumption of material. Since the material was highly valued, this was a very important aspect of the process of production. To handle the material economically was a true proof of skill.

What do the alternating parts of white linen and coloured patterns tell us? At first one can notice the weaver having a high concentration level while weaving the patterns in weft-pattern tabby, type "opphämta". This technique means the weaver cannot automatically shuttle by changing the feet on the tramps and the hands on the raddle. Instead, she has to pick up some of the warp threads by hand in order to create the pattern desired. Weaving the white linen parts between the patterns means, on the other hand, using tabby, the most common and plain weaving technique. There are almost no mistakes in the weaving of the pattern sequences but many of them in the ground weave. In the first case the weaver is concentrated on the skilled and difficult parts of the work; in the latter she eases back while weaving, letting the body find a rhythm for working.

Materials and Colours

Flax was cultivated locally, and it seems as if the linen used in the textiles was the result of cultivating and dressing flax in the households. The process from seeding the flax to the linen yarn ready to be warped and spooled meant a lot of work that took a very long time. When planning textiles one had

Ill. 1: Detail of a "hängkläde", a woven textile hanging along the walls, with a pattern of blue woollen weft. (Photo: Hugo Palmsköld.)

to image the whole process and not only the actual textile production such as weaving. Since the harvest some years was rich and other years not, access to the material varied.

A linen textile has to be handled with care. If, for example, it is washed in too hot water, the glossy surface characterizing the material is destroyed. Thus the linen turns from cool, steady and substantial to a flimsy piece of fabric. The interior textiles bear witness to having been in good care since the material is not damaged. They have not been washed in a wrong way. The owners have taken good care of them, as one does when handling objects highly valued. The skill of weaving, then, is also a skill of handling the product and the material it is made of.

In the process of turning the flax into linen, one of the phases is bleaching the material from a natural beige tone to a silky white one. When weaving a linen fabric without coloured parts, the common method was to bleach the fabric after it had been taken down from the loom. The pieces of cloth were spread out on a lawn suitable for letting the sun bleach the surface. With loops attached to the fabric, wooden sticks helped to keep it in place and stay unwrinkled in the warm and strong sunshine. Weaving a linen fabric with white parts mixed with coloured parts, on the other hand, meant bleaching the linen yarn before transforming it into textiles. Again putting the linen skein in the sunshine was the best method.

The white ground weaving constitutes a contrast to the pattern originally brightly coloured in blue or blue and red. Studying the fabrics today means looking at far more light colours faded by age and use, sometimes having been directly exposed to sunlight.

When the fabric is turned inside out, the original nuances appear as they have been protected. Weaving the patterns means creating a weave with two different sides, since the weft on the backside turns to a negative in comparison to the positive pattern on the right side.

Most of the textile objects have blue linen in their patterns. They may be the older ones, since linen is a domestic material but cotton is not. Comparing linen to cotton requires observing the differences in the surfaces. Where linen is silky and glossy, cotton is dull and does not break the light, making the fabric shine. On the other hand cotton is better when it comes to colours. It is easier to dye cotton than linen and to make the colour fix. That is why the linen patterns are blue and the cotton patterns are red – it is very difficult to dye linen in red. Another difference is how the yarn was spun. Since the linen yarn was a result of the process of cultivating and dressing flax in the households, it was spun on a spinning-wheel or a spindle. The material cotton was desired, as it was bought on skeins or in balls of yarn, ready to be used. Whether it was already coloured in red or dyed after being bought is not clear from the research material.

With cotton the patterns could be varied more than formerly. The skill of combining red and blue for a beautiful result became important besides the skill in creating beautiful and incessantly varied patterns and pattern sequences. Since cotton was considered a more exclusive material, it was handled with care from an economic point of view in the weaving process and the design of the patterns. It is the blue colour that dominates, and the red cotton was used to emphasize details in the patterns as well as the general impression of the weave.

When using blue-dyed wool, prepared in the household, the effect was another than when combining red cotton and blue linen or using only blue linen for patterns. The wool as a material made it possible to dye the yarn in a strong dark blue colour. With this dark blue wool the weaver created a weave with marked contrasts between the dark patterns and the shiny white linen in the ground weave. The pattern stands out, looking like graphic art in black on white paper. This effect made it possible to simplify the patterns so that the pattern sequences could consist of fewer details. On the other hand, it was when using red cotton and blue linen for patterns that the weaver was able to create the most beautiful product. The pattern sequences are full of details, they are placed perfectly in rows, and the colours and the patterns follow in a nice blend of rhythm, pleasant to look at and expressing the skill of the weaver.

Textile Objects for Decoration

Using the textile objects for decoration meant putting them along the walls and the ceiling in a timber cottage open to the roof and with a window placed in the ceiling, a typical farm house in the south of Sweden during the period. The combined living room and kitchen usually had no panels or any other thing to cover the wooden walls and ceiling. The consequences of living everyday life in this kind of room were dust and soot coming from cooking and the open fireplace sticking to the walls, the ceiling, the timber beams, the furniture, the textiles, the objects and the tools belonging to life in a farmhouse. Since the interior textiles were highly valued, they did not belong to everyday decoration. Instead, they were put up together with painted wall-hangings during Christmas and other festive and ceremonial occasions. The whole room was cleaned, and the linen textiles with geometric patterns were put up together with paintings illustrating well-known stories from the Bible. The room was transformed from darkness to light and from almost no colours to shiny white combined with the bright colours of red and blue from the weavings and also green, yellow, orange and blue painted on the wall-hangings. The strictly geometric patterns on the weavings contrasted with the motifs depicted by the paintings. The transformation itself can be seen as a ritual starting from ordinary routines in everyday life, turning to arranging the room for a certain occasion and winding up in celebrating a festival (Bringéus 1982: 22ff).

While starting to weave an interior textile to be part of the room decoration, the creator knew where it was supposed to be placed. In planning the work she could measure the reach, placing the main central pattern sequence where it was supposed to be placed in the interior. It seems that this place was above the cupboard in the corner beside the dining table. When entering the door into the room, visitors could view the whole decoration with woven textiles hanging along the walls (*hängkläden*), from the ceiling (*drättar*), from the edges of protruding shelves and other stationary objects (*lister*) and sometimes over the dining table (*takduk*). Beside the textiles on the walls painted wall-hangings were placed. It must have been an overwhelming sight, representing the skills of the female weavers in the household alongside the economic power used to buy painted wall-hangings from a local painter.

When analyzing the meaning of the decorations one has to consider the parallel visual impressions from the interior textiles and from the painted wall-hangings. Studying textile objects, one has to be aware of the dominance of abstract patterns. One can claim that the technique chosen for textile production sets the limits for what it is possible to create when it comes to patterns. This is true to a point, but there have been other concerns for the weavers to take into consideration while creating. One example is patterns that were named and that were supposed to be used in certain combinations, as a skilled weaver told a collector in 1886. That is to say, there were rules for the weaver to follow when creating a weave. The abstraction of the woven patterns corresponds to the visualisation of stories from the Bible. The first corresponding element is the language of practice, giving form to abstract patterns on textiles, and the latter is the language of religion, visualised and told in a popular form. Possibly the textiles stand for everyday life and the conditions of life structured from a practical point of view. On the

Ill. 2: Bollaltebygget (the name of a cottage) with the interior of today, displayed for visitors. (Photo: Länsmuseet Halmstad/Jan Svensson.)

other hand, perhaps the painted wall-hangings are representations of religious questions concerning human existence, the meaning of life and death and human fate.

Conclusions

In this article I have discussed parts of the process I have gone through in using interior textiles as a scientific source. In my opinion information that cannot be found anywhere else is given by objects. The process of creating a weave is, for example, inscribed in the actual fabric left to be studied and analyzed. Since this kind of skilled production is practically non-verbal, one cannot find any textual sources from the time describing the process. Even if there were such descriptions to read, it would probably be difficult to follow them without having the product to look at to be able to understand the process. In the process of verbalizing descriptions of the actual objects, answering prepared questions, one soon finds out that there are more questions to notice – the objects themselves generate questions. It is important to be aware of this potential that lies in the objects.

To study material objects created in the past is the example for this discussion. But the lack of information from interviews, conversations and text documents is not only a problem when studying history. Even if it is possible to encounter informants asking important questions or doing participant observations interpreting experiences textually, still there are areas not to be verbalized. Some things are not talked about, and some things are expressed by gestures, by glancing, or by mediating through the body, in practice or by using objects. To analyze culture is also to be aware of this kind of communication and to find ways to discover the underlying meaning.

The capacity of generating questions and representing silent communication are two aspects to be aware of when trying to understand materiality. A third point is viewing and analyzing objects as materialized discourses. As the literary theorist Edward Said has pointed out, orientalism is not only to be found articulated in words, but also materialized in books, films, institutions, collections and so on (Said 1993). When analyzing objects one can go the other way around, asking which discourses are to be materialized in them.

The American publisher and social anthropologist Robert Plant Armstrong has analyzed African sculptures in order to find the cultural essence of them. His works are inspired by phenomenological theory, as he says:

> in this philosophy lies the only option open to the anthropologist if he is to […] emerge into a study of man that is blessed with those meanings that do justice to the dignity, the subtlety and richness of man himself (Plant Armstrong 1971: XV).

By studying the things themselves, the sculptures, he finds the essence of them to be concentrated in two words: *intensive continuity* (ibid. 1971). These words also unify the style of the African culture in Plant Armstrong's analysis. His conclusion is that objects have the capacity to concentrate cultural essence, as they are culturally embedded. Another way of putting this is to say that they materialize structures and discourses.

Understanding materiality is a way to overcome the lack of documents and information when studying things as they are. It is to analyze the objects in order to find the communicative dimension that lies in them. Understanding materiality is also an effort to understand the cultural essence of the objects, discussing what cultural structures would be materialized in the objects, in the making of them and in their use.

Notes

1. Every county had its own museum on regional cultural history and art beside Skansen, the Nordic Museum, the Historical Museum and the National Museum, all located in Stockholm.
2. My thesis (in progress) focuses on the production, use and interpretation of this category of interior textiles from the eighteenth and nineteenth centuries. The textiles belong geographically speaking to the province of Halland, on the west coast of Sweden. Starting from the objects themselves, as they appear in museum collections, I try to link close scrutiny of them with material from archives and primary textual sources, to analyze

conditions of their creation and decoration. Aided by theories on phenomenology and materiality my approach is to situate the textiles in suitable contexts and historical times. The most important question is, what did the textile objects mean to those who created them, decorated rooms with them and studied them? This essay is the result of a methodological discussion concerning the material. I am grateful for the proofreading of the article by Timothy Cox, Ph.D.

3 Most of the objects in the regional museums of Sweden and in the Nordic Museum were collected during this period of almost fifty years. When it comes to the textile objects in my study, approximately 60 percent were collected in this first period.

4 Alexis Engdahl was a collector of objects for the Nordic Museum in Stockholm in the 1880s. He travelled in different parts of Sweden to find interesting objects to collect and to document their context in words and by illustrations. During a visit in the southern part of Halland in 1885–1886, he wrote to his principal, Artur Hazelius, the founder of the Nordic Museum and of Skansen. The letters describe the situation of competition among many collectors to find the most fascinating objects. The sellers took advantage of the situation when charging the best price for each object. Engdahl also expresses an anti-Semitic attitude when complaining about "the Jews" from Poland who, according to him, bought everything from the farm households in order to export the objects to earn money by selling them to collectors and museums abroad (letters from Alexis Engdahl to Artur Hazelius, September 6, 1884 and May 12, 1885).

5 Practically speaking the lack of professional full-time employees is another reason. The Regional Museum of Halland in Halmstad was for example run by amateurs in Halland's Museum Association until 1928, when the first professional curator of the museum was employed.

6 The interior textiles were produced locally to be used in the households. They were inscribed in a local tradition of decorating rooms for certain events.

7 I have found a few examples of a white linen warp and a white cotton weft.

References

Museum Collections
Interior textiles (approximately 220 *hängkläden*, *drättar*, *lister* and *takdukar*) in the collections of the Regional Museum in Halmstad.

Archives
The archive of the Nordic Museum: letters from Alexis Engdahl to Artur Hazelius, 1884–1901.

Literature
Arendt, Hannah 1998: *Människans villkor: vita activa*. Göteborg: Daidalos.
Bringéus, Nils-Arvid 1982: *Sydsvenska bonadsmålningar*. Lund: Signum.
Palmsköld, Anneli forthcoming: Textila tolkningar. Om hängkläden, drättar, lister och takdukar. (Thesis in progress.)
Plant Armstrong, Robert 1971: *The Affecting Presence: An Essay in Humanistic Anthropology*. Chicago: University of Illinois Press.
Ricoeur, Paul 1988: *Från text till handling: en antologi om hermeneutik*. Eds: Peter Kemp & Bengt Kristensson. Stockholm, Lund: Symposion.
Said, Edward W. 1993: *Orientalism*. Stockholm: Ordfronts förlag.
Semper, Gottfried 1860: *Die Texile Kunst für sich betrachtet und in Beziehung zur Baukunst*. Frankfurt: Vrl. für Kunst & Wissenschaft.

Anneli Palmsköld is a Ph.D.-student at the University of Lund, working at the Regional Museum of Halmstad, Sweden. Her thesis in progress focuses on the production, use and interpretation of a category of interior textiles from the eighteenth and nineteenth centuries. Starting from the objects themselves she analyzes conditions of their creation and decoration. Aided by theories on phenomenology and materiality the approach is to situate the textiles in suitable contexts and historical times.
(anneli.palmskold@hallmus.se)

CONTESTED MODERNITIES. POLITICS, CULTURE AND URBANISATION IN PORTUGAL
A Case Study from the Greater Lisbon Area

Gisela Welz and Eva Maria Blum

The article analyses a long-term conflict centred on an abandoned shipyard situated across the Tagus from the historical city centre of Lisbon. Since 1999, ambitious plans to build high-rise office towers and luxury apartments on the deserted site polarized politics and public opinion in the area, and local struggles about what to do with this former industrial waterfront became a catalyst for debates that reverberated through the entire country, throwing into sharp relief conflicting cultures of modernity that compete for hegemony in Portuguese society. In our study that spans the years 1999–2007, we consider urban planning and the political controversies spawned by urbanist interventions as a privileged site for the investigation of the cultural construction of modernities.

Keywords: modernity, urban planning, political culture, Portugal, Lisbon

> Moderna Almada [...]
> E tens força e tens beleza
> E desde que Abril surgiu
> És a cidade portuguesa
> Das que mais evoluiu[1]

These lines from the song composed for the "Marchas Populares" of the year 2004 in the Portuguese municipality of Almada celebrate the community's "force and beauty". Such popular marches are annual public events in many Portuguese towns and cities, occasions on which marching bands, parades of local organisations, song contests, and folklore performances transform streets and squares into open-air stages, and serve to coalesce a fierce communal pride. The lines quoted above emphasize that since the revolution of April 1974 that overthrew the dictatorship of the Right, no other town in Portugal has undergone comparable growth and development as Almada on the southern shore of the Tagus estuary, just opposite of the city of Lisbon.[2] Other stanzas of the song go on to rhapsodize the progressive character of the town, and emphasize that it is well-governed, has modern infrastructure, and offers employment to its residents. While it may appear odd at first sight that modernity is positively invoked as a matter of pride and achievement in a traditionalist cultural format, our essay will proceed to show how the community's engagement with modernity articulates its history and expresses its specifically local "tradition of modernisation". Indeed, the Marchas Populares are no relic of traditional popular culture either, but are an invented tradition of the 1930s[3] that later on was promoted by the regime of the Estado Novo as part of its policy of folklorization, aiming for the creation of a nationalist cultural idiom based on an idealized Portuguese folk culture.

The emblematic modernity cheered on by the urban working-class celebrants in the street of Almada on June 23rd 2004, however, was not uncontested. Rather, another, radically different vision of modern urban life was competing with the communal pride of the children and grandchildren of migrants from rural Portugal who came here to work in the factories and who in the majority support the Communist-lead local government. This other vision emerged when the Lisnave Docks, one of the largest shipyards in the world located on the Tagus shore of Almada, specializing in oil tanker repair, was slated to shut down during the 1990s because its operations were going to be shifted to another area, further south on the Atlantic Coast. The huge dock land area situated across the Tagus from the historical city centre of Lisbon that fell into disuse at the beginning of 2001 became a catalyst for conflicts that reverberated through the entire country.

As early as 1999, ambitious plans to build high-rise office towers and luxury apartments on this site polarized politics and public opinion far beyond the Greater Lisbon Area. These plans engaged a vision of modernity that endeavoured to put Almada – and with it, the entire Lisbon area – on a global map of world cities that serve as nodes of the international service economy and financial sector. In our essay, we will employ the increasingly heated and still ongoing conflict over what to do with the abandoned shipyard as a case-in-point, arguing that it throws into sharp relief conflicting cultures of modernity that compete for hegemony in Portuguese society.

Modernisation in Social Discourse

The following article reports findings from an extended fieldwork project conducted in the Greater Lisbon Area from 2004 until 2007.[4] We consider urban planning, and the political controversies spawned by urbanist interventions, a privileged site for the investigation of "glocal" practices. According to Roland Robertson (1998), globalization processes are always appropriated, resisted, subverted, and modified in local settings. Depending on differences in historically generated cultural circumstances and in political and economic frameworks, the effects

Ill.1: View of the abandoned dry dock of the Lisnave Shipyards in Almada across the Tagus River from Lisbon. (Photo: Eva Maria Blum.)

vary considerably. Robertson emphasizes the fact that as a consequence of globalization, "the local" is not obliterated but rather reinvented anew. As a country on the margins of Europe, both geographically and, for a long time also socio-economically, Portugal lends itself especially well to inquiries into the cultural construction of modernity. To pursue an "anthropology of modernity" (Kahn 2001) means to resolutely turn away from an understanding of anthropology as the study of the pre-modern and the traditional, that has constituted the original impetus of anthropological research. While modern societies have been of interest to anthropologists only because of the relics of traditional cultures they harboured and the pockets of not-yet-modern practices left by the onslaught of modernisation, the anthropology of modernity that emerged internationally in the 1980s focuses on the cultural dimensions of those institutions, discourses, and practices that are considered modern: the state and its bureaucracies, science and technology, infrastructure and planning, medicine and education, the economy and the military (see Rabinow 1989; Appadurai 1996). More precisely, an anthropology of modernity implies to inquire into how social actors make modernity relevant in their own lives, and to make modern subjectivities, the social imaginaries of modernity, and the transformations of social agency in modern societies, topical in anthropology. (See Frykman & Löfgren 1987; Herzfeld 1992; Geertz 1995.) This has also triggered self-reflexive inquiries into the role of ethnography as a form of modern knowledge production (Marcus & Fischer 1986; Clifford & Marcus 1986).

In our project, we looked at the region of Lisbon as one experiencing a spectacular and accelerated growth and expansion. Many of the dynamics that shape the Lisbon area can be observed in similar form in other southern European countries as well. As such, Portugal is particularly suited as a comparison case to other circum-Mediterranean countries, especially Greece and Spain, with whom it shares some of the same problematics of a rapid transition from a primarily agrarian economy, the legacy of authoritarian political rule and the achievement of democratization, and the decisive influence of European integration. Even though political analysts and social scientists in Portugal readily place their society within that frame of reference, we would also like to point out some aspects that make Portugal a special case.

For many decades, the modernisation of Portuguese society was not an anthropological concern, but considered the domain of sociology. Sociology as a discipline did not come into its own until after restrictions on the critical inquiry into Portuguese society were lifted after the April Revolution of 1974 (see Viegas & Costa 2000). Conversely, anthropology came into being in Portugal as a "nation-building" discipline in the last quarter of the nineteenth century, along the lines of ethnological and folklorist endeavours in other European nation states that were concerned with salvaging and documenting authentic folk culture, and enlisting oral traditions and material culture in the construction of a national identity.[5] In the twentieth century, ethnological research on the traditional cultures and folk arts of rural Portugal remained an important concern, especially throughout the rule of the fascist "Estado Novo". After 1974, the discipline was able to develop new research concerns and to engage more intensely with theoretical discussions of the international anthropological arena. (See Branco 1982.) Since then, anthropology's former engagement with defining, conserving and representing traditional Portuguese culture itself has become an important topic of contemporary researchers who inquire into anthropology's role in the creation of museum collections (see Bouquet 1999) and the folklorization of expressive cultures (see El-Shawan Castelo-Branco & Branco 2003). More recently, the effect of the historical legacy of colonialism and the recent changes associated with globalization also come into the purview of Portuguese anthropologists[6] who started to study immigration, multiculturalism, and the social problems of the urban peripheries.

"Modern Almada": Migration, Industrialization, and Suburbanization

Almada is an exceptional community. Yet, even in its extremes, it reflects developments that are typical for all of Portugal. Industrialization has transformed Almada and neighbouring communities since the 1940s, making it a magnet for poor migrants from the countryside, and later, for returnees from the former colonies. Its urban sprawl was generated by the immense population growth and the resultant, largely unchecked development of residential construction that started in the 1960s. In the last decades, the metropolitan area of Lisbon, and with it Almada, were attracting hundreds of thousands of people who left their homes in the depressed agricultural regions of inland Portugal and migrated to the industrialized areas near the coast, clustering around the port cities and metropolitan centres on the Atlantic Ocean. This still-ongoing process of "littoralization", meaning the concentration of by now 80 percent of the Portuguese population in the coastal plain adjacent to the Atlantic littoral (see Machado & Costa 2000), coupled with labour migration to northern Europe and other overseas countries, led to the abandonment and "desertification" of inland agricultural economies. By the same token, it created an immense urbanisation pressure, especially in the Lisbon and Porto metropolitan areas where today more than half of the Portuguese population resides. Situated across the river from Lisbon, Almada is an urban centre in its own right, but for decades it served as a valve to absorb the residential overflow of Lisbon and the areas north of the Tagus. The opening of the huge Tagus bridge in 1966, connecting Lisbon with the peninsula of Setubal on which Almada is situated, was instrumental in this development.

The entire area administered by the municipality of Almada which stretches from the Atlantic coast beaches of Caparica to the heavily industrialized southern shore of the Tagus estuary, and incorporates numerous former villages, small towns and agricultural holdings, was shaped by this process. Slums and shantytowns with stark poverty were its most extreme effects. Rapidly built housing projects and high-rise blocks were created to ameliorate this situation, without any systematic framework of urban planning.[7] Large parts of the territory of the

Ill. 2: Billboard advertising the construction of a low-income housing project in Almada. In the background, Almada city blocks and the Cristo Rey monument are visible. (Photo: Eva Maria Blum.)

municipality of Almada are considered suburban, according to Portuguese terminology. What is called "suburbanisation" in Portugal does not necessarily refer to single-family homes for the middle class outside the city, but is often taken to mean substandard housing in blocks of buildings, considered rife with social problems, constructed on the urban peripheries. After 1974, state-induced slum-clearance programmes relocated many slum dwellers to such housing blocks.

The revolution of April 25, 1974, that did away with the political repression of the Salazar regime and ended the disastrous involvement in the overseas colonial wars, was faced with the immense challenge of eradicating social inequality in a country that was considered one of the poorest in Europe, with an illiteracy rate of more than one quarter of the population as late as 1970. The democratization of the country, and the opening-up of society, allowing all sectors of the population access to education and social mobility, which since the mid-1970s was made possible by the April Revolution, continue to be a source of pride for large parts of the population even today, more than 30 years later.

In Almada, the Municipal Museum dedicates a considerable portion of its permanent exhibit on the past and present of the community to the local events of the Revolution and the contributions of the industrial and shipyard workers of Almada to the overthrow. The April Revolution thus is as much a reference point for collective memory and local identities as it was the most decisive catalyst for the

Ill. 3: A panel at the exhibit commemorating the 30th anniversary of the April Revolution in 2004 at the local historical museum. The exhibit was created by the municipality and focused on local events in Almada under the title "To give wings to dreams". (Photo: Eva Maria Blum.)

modernisation of Portuguese society. The modernisation trajectory of Portuguese society is marked by another, equally important passage point, Portugal's accession to the European Community in 1986. The accession to the European Community is generally considered to mark the point in time when agriculture declined considerably, and industrial production decreased in importance relative to the service sector.

Already in the 1970s, service professions started to increase considerably in Almada. In the course of the 1980s, the percentage of those employed in industrial production decreased from 40 to 30 percent of local employment. Still, among those, the workers in the shipyards constructing and repairing seagoing vessels constituted the strongest group, with 57 percent of all industrial workers employed in Almada in 1984. This particular industrial sector underwent massive changes due to globalization pressures. The Lisnave Shipyards, situated in the Cacilhas section of Almada right across from Lisbon, fell victim to the restructuring of its owner company, and one of the biggest dry docks for oil tankers in the world closed down in 2000, with far-ranging negative consequences for the local economy and employment situation.

An Incomplete Modernity?

In Portugal, society's engagement with globalization is interpreted against the backdrop of a specific modernization trajectory in the twentieth century, and indeed, also against the backdrop of an imperial colonial history reaching many centuries back. At the beginning of the twenty-first century, many Portuguese authors in the social sciences enlist classical modernization theories to assess the progress their society has made, especially during the past 30 years since the Revolution. Modernisation is considered to be a standardized process following a normative course for which the societies of northern Europe serve as a model. Analysts of the Portuguese modernisation process compare their country with other, more longstanding members of the European Union that are considered to be "further developed" and serve as a standard against which the development of their own society ought to be measured. This type of comparison is a major theme in social science discourse in Portugal and can be considered quite influential outside of academia as well. In addition, a diachronic comparison of the Portugal of the past with that of the present is often invoked, with backwardness, traditionalism, authoritarianism, and the subjugation to centralized power as the most important traits of the past from which the present needs to distinguish itself – and sometimes, in the observers' opinions, does so only incompletely.

While many changes started in the 1960s and were accelerated by the achievements of the 1974 revolution, the process of modernisation is considered to have been speeded up considerably by accession to the European Community in 1986, with growing prosperity, the emergence of a middle class, the pluralization of society, and the spread of mass consumption as the most important changes. Ever since, the elimination of backwardness has become the most frequently voiced political promise, prevalent among all political parties across the spectrum (see Barreto 2000: 69). Even though experts attest to Portugal's impressive pace in attaining structural change, they are also very much aware of the fact that the process does not follow the model set by other societies to the letter, and that many goals still remain to be attained. For that reason, the pertinent social science literature and political analyses in the media continue to speak of the modernisation process in Portugal as being "imbalanced" (Barreto 2000: 68f), or else of an "incomplete modernity" (Viegas & Costa 2000: 6). This discourse relies on conventional models of modernisation and views the course of Portuguese societies primarily in terms of "deficits". Since EU accession, the multitude of subsidy programmes and infrastructural funds, that Portugal has been able to benefit from, has in a paradoxical way reinforced this self-image of Portuguese society as being in a position of lagging behind and having to catch up. Surely, the orientation towards Europe and towards the European Union is a very recent and in some ways still fragile development, fraught with difficulties in terms of fulfilling conditions set for the national economic and social policies. Yet, to talk of the country as being "na cauda da Europa", the rearguard of Europe, is widespread among journalists and politicians. In some cases, this serves not only to scandalize delays and deficits in developing society, but expresses nostalgia and mourning over the loss of a past "historical greatness" (see Lourenço 1997). This refers to the former hegemonial position as the centre of a large colonial empire which today has given way to a geographically and economically peripheral position within Europe.

Anthropologists in recent years have been exceedingly critical of the application of classical modernization theory when employed to assess "a society's progress", particularly in peripheral and non-Western societies. Indeed, to use institutions and values of northern European and North American cultures as a yardstick against which to measure the modernity of societies, tends to freeze most other societies in positions of "not-yet" or "not quite", and to see them primarily in terms of lags and deficits. Instead of the teleological narrative of modernization, anthropologists propose to acknowledge "alternative constructions of modernity in the sense of moral-political projects that seek to control their own present and future" (Ong 1999: 23; see also Ong 2001) rather than straining to conform with criteria and scales imposed from the outside. The notion that there is not one universal type of modernity but rather "multiple modernities" (see Hannerz 1996; Kahn 2001) is an attractive one, as it brings within the purview of anthropology all those non-traditional social formations that anthropologists would hesitate to call modern according to a narrowly conceived Euro-American model.[8] However, the anthropological critique of modernization theory is mostly concerned with chiding Western social scientists as being politically incorrect by not acknowledging non-Western societies' ability to determine their own path into and through modernity. What these critiques to some extent obviate is that today, the image of an ideal type of linear progress is most prevalent and effective in non-Western societies themselves, firmly embedded in their political discourses and cultures of expertise. It is no longer the social scientists from abroad, but local analysts, experts and decision makers who enlist this powerful trope of the modern. Cultural anthropologist Vassos Argyrou has repeatedly pointed out that modernity is not a goal to be reached but rather an identity that non-Western societies "tie themselves to [...] and submit in this way to other, more powerful societies" (1996: 1). In our paper, we explore how in Portugal, this modern identity is engaged by social actors in a variety of ways to pursue their political goals and cultural objectives.

Torres de Manhattan em Cacilhas: Towers of Contention

"Torres de Manhattan em Cacilhas" was the headline of the Portuguese newspaper *Expresso* on April 24, 1999. This marked the beginning of a protracted conflict about the future of the Lisnave Shipyards, at that point in time still operating but their closure considered imminent. The media attacked the plans proposed by the owner of the land, the real estate fund Fundo Margueira Capital, to build high-rise buildings on the site of the former docks in Cacilhas, the part of Almada where the Lisnave was located on the river front. The ambitious plans called for a spectacular project with skyscrapers of up to 80 floors, on a site directly across the river from the historical old town of Lisbon. The newspaper's polemic enlisted the image of the Manhattan skyline[9] that had been thrown into the discussion at the very first press conference on the project in 1999 by the Lady Mayor of Almada, Maria Emília Neto de Sousa, who from the beginning fiercely opposed the plans. In the years to come, she would emerge as a formidable enemy for Ricardo Nunes, the managing director of the Margueira Fund, who was passionately committed to transforming the former industrial river front into a glamorous, internationally renowned urbanist project. His opponent, the mayor, is quoted in the newspaper as fearing that high-rises would keep the sunlight away from the community of Almada. "They are going to steal the sky that belongs to the people of Almada," she is reported to have said. Her rhetoric was well-chosen to mobilize popular sentiment. Opposition to the project that was called "megalomaniac" or even "monstrous" quickly began to be voiced in the public arena far beyond Almada. Some critics would focus on the vicinity of the project to the architectural heritage of Lisbon, arguing that it was misplaced so close to the old urban centre, others feared that the aesthetic impact on the southern riverside of the Tagus would be disastrous.[10] The highest structure on the peninsular shore opposite of Lisbon had been, uncontested since the 1960s, the world-famous figure of Cristo Rey. That high-rise buildings – even at a considerable distance – should compete with it was a provocation.

At first sight, then, the disproportionately adverse reaction to the plan, and the vicious polemics that developed between the protagonists on both sides, are similar to comparable antagonisms in other cities around the world. Plans to erect high-rise buildings close to or in historical city centres often lead to extremely polarized disputes between supporters and opponents (see Rodenstein 2006). In Portugal as well, the question whether skyscrapers of such scale are compatible with the urban building tradition of the country – and with its culture in general – was hotly debated in the media and public fora. However, a closer scrutiny reveals that the incendiary quality of the conflict had less to do with the height of the planned buildings but with irreconcilable differences in the politics and cultural orientations of those involved on opposite sides. In order to better understand this conflict, it is useful to look into the history and especially into the economics of the site.

In 1993, it first became public knowledge that the corporation who owns the Lisnave would close down the site at Cacilhas, consolidating its operations at the Setnave shipyards to the south of the peninsula at the port of Setubal. The municipal government refused to accept that decision and demanded that the jobs should remain in Almada. The municipality had shortly before passed a zoning ordinance for the entire community that defined the site as "industrial" and thereby excluded future uses as residential or office space. However, the central government who had the final say on the zoning ordinance disagreed with this declaration and cut the area of the Lisnave Shipyards out of the municipal document. The municipality saw this intervention by the central government as an attack on the community's lawful right to legislate building zones within its territory, and promptly filed suit at the highest administrative court of the country. Independent municipalities, and elections for municipal officers and town parliaments, are very recent institutions in Portugal and did not exist before 1976. The political figure of the municipal government with a measure of independence from the central state is viewed as a progressive achievement that was made possible by the 1974 revolution, and any attack on the sovereignty of local power is considered onerous.

It can be assumed that the central government had moved against the continuation of the industrial use of the site as declared by the community's zoning ordinance, in order to leave the issue of the future use of the shipyard site open. Alternatives to industrial uses had to be considered, because the outgoing company had saddled the state with a considerable financial burden. In the 1960s, the fascist regime of the Estado Novo had given over the area of the docks to the Lisnave[11] company on the condition that if the company ceased operations on the site, the terrain would revert to state ownership and the state, in turn, would recompense the company for the investments it had made on the site for the erection of structures. When in the early 1990s, the decision was made to close down the Lisnave Shipyards, it was determined that the Portuguese state would have to pay a compensation of EUR 210 Million to the company. In order to raise this sum, the state and a number of banks created the above mentioned real estate fund Fundo Margueira Capital, in which the Portuguese state holds the majority, and charged it with the task of developing a highly profitable real estate project on the site. This is where Ricardo Nunes – and the architects he committed to his plans – comes in.

While the leading politicians of the municipality of Almada belong to or have a strong affinity to the Communist Party and consider themselves heirs of the April 1974 revolution, the protagonists of the real estate fund represent a fundamentally different political culture. They carry on the tradition of an entrepreneurial elite that – while it supported the Revolution because the economic policies of the Estado Novo were no longer in their best interests – has mostly opposed the reforms and measures of post-revolutionary governments, in particular the abandoning of Portugal's overseas possessions and the policy of dispossessing privately-owned companies.[12] Adherents of this camp had always been unequivocally pro Europe, while the Communist Party had been against Portugal's accession to the EU in 1986.[13] While this entrepreneurial elite today holds a neoliberal view of the role of the state, the political milieu that the municipal rulers of Almada belong to regards the state as being the guarantor of the welfare of the people.

Ricardo Nunes, who at the time of these events was managing director of the real estate fund, had no connections to Almada prior to the project. He lived in Lisbon for much of his life and shared with the educated classes of the city a denigrating attitude towards people living south of the river Tagus. Other experts interviewed in the course of our research affirm that Lisbonians generally consider those on the other side as backward and provincial. Nunes himself in an interview[14] called the residents of Almada "former peasants who had been transformed into factory workers" and entered into polemics against the communist-lead town halls of the municipalities on the other side. He accused the municipal government of Almada of having lost touch with present-day developments. In particular, he claims that they have not realized yet that Portugal has entered the post-industrial age:

> The tragedy is that these town halls are trying to carry on the legacy of 1975 when the communists took power in these communities [...] They did so democratically because the population was working class, ex-peasants who had become factory workers. But the industrial revolution has come to an end. There is still industrial production, yet it does not operate with people anymore, but with machines. This is why it is no longer necessary that the political leaders in these communities defend the workers – simply because there are no workers any more. That's over. The society we are building today is a leisure society. [15]

When the municipal government of Almada rejected his project, he saw this as evidence of their backwardness. What he did not see, because he was caught in his own prejudiced world view, was that the municipal elite was far from backward. They were very much aware of the fact that de-industrialisation had become a dominant economic process, that the economic paradigms had changed, and that they needed to embark on a new type of modernization strategy in order to maintain and increase the welfare of Almada's population. Because of his preconceived notions of the motivations of the mayor and her supporters, he failed to take their opposition seriously. Because of his deeply ingrained anti-communism, he was also unable to realize that the communists, too, saw that globalization and Europeanization were processes that they could not escape or obviate, and that they needed to find a new compromise to pursue their goal of creating a progressive society.

"Portugal dos Pequenitos": A Cultural Conflict

The closure of the Lisnave Docks had originally been scheduled for 1996. When Nunes and the real estate fund were charged with developing the site and began working in 1995, they had anticipated an early start for their urbanization project. However, the closing-down was delayed twice, until at last, the shipyards ceased to operate at the end of 2000. Before it closed down, one and a half thousand workers still worked there.[16]

Charged with launching a project to rebuild the site before 2002, Ricardo Nunes quickly took action. When the plans developed by the first architect commissioned by him did not please him, he began to pursue a vision of his own: He wanted high-rises. He refreshed old contacts he had to Hong Kong and Macau, started to network with the protagonists of the London Docklands project, and was able to win one of the most prestigious Portuguese architectural firms, the studio of Manuel Graça Dias and Egas José Viera, known for their unconventional designs, for the project. Nunes envisioned "a complete urban formation" for fifteen thousand new residents, including an entirely new infrastructure and "attrac-

Ill. 4: The emblematic gantry arch still dominates the site of the former Lisnave Shipyards and is clearly visible even from across the river. None of the proposals to convert the site to new uses dared to suggest a removal of the "porticus". (Photo: Eva Maria Blum.)

tions" such as a huge shopping mall. The architects suggested that it should be connected to Almada by way of an elliptical avenue. At the centre of the new project were high-rise towers of more than 80 floors. Clearly, under the condition of having to create a high financial return, the decision for sky scrapers represented a smart solution of multiplying the number of square metres of residential and commercial spaces that would be produced. Yet, for Nunes, the Towers as they were going to be called represented not merely an economically profitable strategy. Rather, he was inspired and even driven by the mission to bestow high-rises on the Lisbon area. A new city to rise like a Phoenix from the ashes and to counteract the banality of the endless suburbs, modelled after the great metropolises of the world such as Chicago, Singapore and Hong Kong, was his intention.[17] The last November edition of the weekly newspaper Expresso in 2000 contained a poster and a brochure on the project "Torres de Manhattan em Cacilhas". It was titled "Eppur si muove" – taking as a cue Galileo's famous saying "And yet it moves". The brochure goes on to say – in Portuguese – "eve-rything is in motion, is developing around us. There is progress". The text was also published on the website of the project. It hails the new promise of overcoming the evils of the industrial age with the new vision of a leisure society and a better future for everybody. "The Towers of Almada will have the force of what the future will be. They are a commitment to the evolutionary trajectory of development and progress."[18] The zone of the Margueira, once one of industrial pollution, so it promises, will become one of fresh air and clear views. Only the high rise constructions will allow Almada to enjoy once again the spectacular beauty of the riverside landscape from which it had been cut off by the Lisnave docks.

In an interview published on December 7th, 2000, in the regional newspaper *Jornal Outra Banda*, Ricardo Nunes claims that the Towers will have an enormous aesthetic presence and are a symbol for modernity. He rejects the interviewer's criticism that they clash with the texture of the built environment along the southern riverfront, and claims that the towers, on the contrary, respect what he calls the memory of the locality which he characterizes as a site known for technological innovations. Such a daring solution would put Lisbon on the map of European metropolises.

One of the leading firms in corporate consulting in Portugal had been commissioned by Nunes to develop a feasibility study on the economic potential of the project. The author of the study, the renowned economist Ernâni Lopes, strongly proposed to Nunes the creation of a new urban region joining both sides of the Tagus estuary. This metropolitan area, composed of Lisbon proper and the municipalities and areas south of the river, would then become a veritable global city, able to compete with other European urban regions for attention and investments. The project, initially known as "Elipse", taking its name from the beltway that would connect it to the rest of Almada, was given a new title, "Ulissul", an artificial composite name joining Lissabon and "sul", the South, with a reference to the mythical founder of the City, Ulysses. The rebuilding of the former Lisnave shipyards in Cacilhas thereby became just one element in a much larger plan that aimed for a comprehensive strategy for the entire Lisbon Area, integrating Lisbon with the southern side of the estuary where Almada is situated.

When opposition to the project massed, Nunes became increasingly polemical and topped his earlier plans with an alternative project that included one structure of 500 m and another of 350 m,[19] modelled after similar projects in Shanghai and elsewhere. Opponents of his vision were derided by him as the lobby of the "tijolinhos" – in Portuguese this means "little bricks". While this is the conventional building material of small structures, Nunes drew the analogy to criticize what he considered the narrow mindedness of his opponents. But in order to launch the project, the Fundo Margueira Capital needed not just the consent, but the active participation of the municipality of Almada. However, the Lady Mayor and the officials of the municipal government sternly refused to negotiate. Without their support, Nunes was threatened to become a lonely fighter for a lost cause. In the interview conducted with him in the context of our research, he himself considered the community's unwillingness to even discuss the project to some extent as politically motivated. Having vowed to fight for the jobs of the departing shipyard, the local political leaders could hardly enter into negotiations about an urbanization project on the site of the shipyards as long as they were still operating and when presumably some jobs could still be saved. Otherwise, they would have lost credibility with their voters. Also, so Nunes suspected, they were not happy about the prospect of the creation of an entirely new, largely middle-class residential area, adding ten or even fifteen thousand new residents who would most likely not vote for the Communist Party, thereby endangering the power base of the Municipal Chamber of Almada.

He also interpreted the sustained opposition to the project as a cultural conflict, proclaiming himself a "cultural crusader":

This is first and foremost a cultural question. I believe that the Towers represent a challenge to their modesty, their smallness. They feel that to build these towers right in front of their noses attacks their smallness. In the North, in Anglo-Saxon and Saxon countries, they have towers because they feel confirmed by them in their sense of greatness. Here, in the South, we have developed a culture of smallness, of being satisfied with being small, of not wanting to offend.[20]

He contends that in order to enter the European stage and to compete with other countries as an equal, Portugal will have to abandon this traditional mentality. In the metropolitan area of the country's capital, there is a need for symbols of growth and greatness and this is what the "vertical configuration" of his visionary skyscrapers promise, so he claims. Sardonically, he associates the opposition of the municipality to his plans with their wish to remain moored in a "Portugal dos Pequenitos". This "country of the small people" is not just a metaphor – it is a theme park built during the regime of the Estado Novo, consisting of miniaturized tableaux of all of Portugal's towns and cities. However, in contemporary discourse,[21] the "Portugal dos Pequenitos" is often used metaphorically along the same lines that

Ricardo Nunes employed it in the interview within the framework of our research. It criticizes a traditional tendency of Portuguese social actors to "think small" and not to have the courage to embark on big endeavours. As such, this smallish Portugal contrasts with the expansive colonial empire of past centuries, and is invoked by those political actors who bemoan the loss of historical greatness that the decolonization to their minds represents.

The Demise of "Ullisul" and the Rise of the "Cidade de Agua"

Exchanges between Nunes and the political leadership of Almada became increasingly acerbic. Both sides enlisted the media and the internet, the Fundo Margueira also used conventional advertising campaigns.[22] While Nunes did not hesitate to call the municipality's methods "Stalinist",[23] the Lady Mayor firmly declared her defiance against the top-down "dictatorial" stance of the real estate fund: "This is not the Latin America of the generals".[24] The Fundo Margueira Capital had been installed by the Ministry of Finances, but openly declared support by the central government was conspicuously absent. This is the more surprising against the backdrop of how the government conducted the huge construction effort on the site of the 1998 Expo that Lisbon hosted. Then, the state took on an entrepreneurial role and lifted any restrictions on development rapidly and easily, so that an entirely new quarter of the city on the site of a formerly industrial waterfront on the northern shore of the Tagus River was created within the space of a few years.[25]

When the Lisnave Docks were about to go out of business at the end of 2000, the local parliament of Almada took action and decided to advertise an international architectural competition for developing the waterfront. The "intervention area" mapped out for this new project included the former Lisnave site, but was much larger, including an area of more than 100 hectares of the neighbouring quarters of Cacilhas and Cova de Piedade, two parts of Almada that included old village centres, industrial areas, and modern housing developments of the 1960s and 1970s. This decision completely ignored the existing proposal by the Fundo Margueira Capital, and when Nunes submitted his plans for the Towers to the municipality for approval in February 2001, it was voted down promptly by the municipality. Meanwhile, the Lady Mayor had met with the Minister of Finances, his ministry originally having commissioned Nunes and the real estate fund with developing the site. Also, José Sócrates, the then Minister of Planning and the Environment who would later become Prime Minister, issued an official declaration in the aftermath of the Lady Mayor's meeting with representatives of the state. In the press release, he unequivocally rejected the plan of the Towers arguing that the huge financial debt that the government had incurred with the closing of the Lisnave should not be paid for by abandoning basic principles of city planning and zoning.

In May 2001, the competition for an architectural plan for the new intervention area, now called "Frente Ribeirinha Nascente", the emerging river front, was internationally advertised. The groundwork had been laid by a highly professional team of civil servants working for the municipality of Almada, consisting of urban planners, engineers, and environmental experts. This team had also developed a unique methodology of having all stakeholders including the residents participate in the planning process. Instead of the top-down planning strategy that Nunes had tried to implement, a participatory project development was envisioned. In the summer of that year, Nunes conceded defeat and left his position as managing director.[26] As it would turn out, relations between the Fundo Margueira and the municipality later improved, and to this date, the new management and the municipal government are cooperating well. In October 2002, the winners of the competition were made public. It was an international architectural consortium, consisting of the Portuguese architectural firm Santa Rita Architects, the British-Portuguese company W.S. Atkins who are known for their expertise in decontaminating former industrial sites, and the internationally renowned British star architect Richard Rogers. At the first discussion forum with local residents, Rogers showed his talent for publicity when he said that now, the site would no longer be transformed into a "Manhattan", but perhaps in its place, a new "Venice" on the Tagus would emerge.

It is important to note the elaborated set of negotiations, discussion fora, and meetings between citizens and the architects established for this project is not legally binding in Portugal. The law merely requires that completed plans have to be made accessible to the public and a public hearing has to be held. With its emphasis on bottom-up participation and the inclusion of all stakeholders including the real estate fund in the planning process, the municipal administration took up a tradition of civil society-oriented urban planning that had emerged with critical planners and architects in opposition to the regime of the Estado Novo during the 1960s. After the revolution, instruments of grassroot participation were often used in the slum clearance projects that created new housing for the poor, and to some extent, became staples in the training of young planners and architects at the universities.[27]

The new plan for rebuilding the Lisnave site and revitalising the adjacent parts of Almada was made public in 2005 under the title "Cidade de Agua".[28] The local parliament had allowed for a building density that would enable the production of one million square metres of build-up space. Nunes, by comparison, had aimed for two million square metres. Yet, even the new plan would not be able to completely renounce high-rise buildings. Indeed, it will comprise a number of buildings of close to 120 metres height, that is, about 35 floors, and is planned for a total population of twelve thousand new inhabitants, little less than what Nunes and his architects Graça Dias and Viera had in mind. The Water City will preserve the original channels and basins of the docks and augment them with gardens and parks. Fifty percent of the buildings are going to be reserved for residential uses, thirty percent for office spaces and commerce, nine percent each for culture and education and for uses by the community, the remaining two percent for maritime functions. What distinguishes the Water City from the earlier plans proposed by Nunes is that it is much better articulated with the existing city space of Almada and that it has a strong ecological component which was lacking in the earlier proposals.

While it is to be expected that most of the apartments in the Cidade de Agua will be beyond the economic means of the average resident of Almada, the project is not being opposed by the population. At the initial public meeting where the plan was presented, the residents who were present appeared to welcome the project. A positive aspect for the residents is the fact that the proposed plan will allow for unrestricted access to the waterfront. A network of pedestrian walkways and a promenade on the riverfront is an integral part of the new plan. When the Lisnave was opened in the 1960s, the residents of Almada were effectively cut off from using the riverside where before many local uses such as boating and a public beach had existed. The plan for the "Cidade de Agua" now promises to return the riverfront to the people.[29]

The municipality of Almada is particularly committed to the creation of employment opportunities on the new site. While the Margueira Fund is thinking of creating a business district for global corporations, coupled with administrative units of the central government, the municipal government is working towards developing a number of cultural institutions that will address the new residents and office workers as well as the resident population of Almada: A cultural centre for the entire region that will host exhibitions, events, and concerts, a library, and a museum devoted to the local tradition of shipbuilding. The political leadership of Almada is also negotiating with the Universidade Nova of Lisbon which has an antenna in Almada and may open another small campus on the Lisvnave site. In the adjoining quarter of Cova de Piedade, a local cultural centre with bookshops, art galleries, cafés, exhibition halls, and rooms to be used by local associations and civil society groups, is also envisioned. This strong emphasis on making cultural events accessible to the entire population, indeed, is not a new policy of the community that was invented for the Cidade de Agua. The municipality has an impressive track record of acquiring historic buildings within its territory and converting them to public use. Thereby, a number of small museums has been developed within the city limits of Almada. The town is also well known throughout the region and beyond for its very active cultural life, hosting one of Portugal's most important annual theatre festivals. A new element in the community's policies, however, is a strong emphasis on environmental issues and the commitment to sustainable urban development. Almada is currently developing its own Agenda-21 strategy.[30]

The commitment of the political leaders of the community to the Cidade de Agua project implies a new orientation, indeed, a new definition of what they mean by "modern Almada". The modernity that they are striving to create for their community is quite different from earlier notions of progress by industrialisation, infrastructure, and adequate housing. Unlike their former opponent, the inventor of the Torres project, they have been able to adopt new goals and find a compromise that, so they hope, will allow them to both ensure the welfare of the population, and to hold on to their political power base in the municipality. Globalization, so they believe, requires of the local government to take responsibility for economic growth and the environment alike, for health and well-being as well as for social integration. They profess to act locally while thinking globally. The three main elements of this new concept of a modern Almada, namely public investments in cultural politics, sustainable and environment-friendly development, and a strengthening of civil society, of course, strongly resonate with major elements of the EU's agenda for European integration. The municipality is actively seeking cooperation with other towns and cities throughout Europe and making use of the existing frameworks for funding and networking, offered by the EU, to further its goals. The new modernisation strategy of Almada is a glocalized practice that integrates non-local, European elements with a specifically local landscape of historically invested experiences and a political culture shaped by the liberation from dictatorship.

Conclusion

We had started our research project with the assumption that in modern societies, architecture as well as urban and regional planning serve as arenas of discourse where the meaning of modernity is being negotiated between various sets of actors. Previous studies by anthropologists had suggested this assumption (see Holston 1989; Rabinow 1989; Berg, Linde-Laursen & Löfgren 2000). It turned out that Portugal is particularly suited for inquiries into the role of architecture in the shaping of society. Certainly, there are obvious reasons why planning and construction are considered important activities in Portuguese society, as the still-ongoing littoralization, the after-effects of uncontrolled urban and suburban development, the often equally disastrous consequences of tourism, and the management of the immense architectural heritage of historic towns and villages all present huge challenges to architects and planners. Yet, beyond their narrowly defined professional role, architects and planners in Portugal are respected as public intellectuals, they regularly write full-page articles in newspapers of national distribution, and are invited to deliver social commentary on the radio and in television.

Our research focussed on the struggles surrounding the deserted docks and yards of the former Lisnave Shipyards, dominated by the "porticus" of the huge gantry that can be seen all the way from Lisbon, spanning the years from 1999 until today. As we have seen, asymmetries between social actors involved in such an arena – local and central governments and their bureaucracies, experts in the fields of planning, architecture, engineering, and environmental affairs, big corporations and small and medium sized companies, NGOs, citizens' groups, media, and other civil-society actors – have to do with differences in the political and economic power they hold. However, their power to shape the direction of a modernization process also rests on their ability to mobilize cultural meanings, and to employ cultural strategies successfully, in order to achieve authority and resonance for their objectives. Following a conceptual move suggested by Anna Tsing (2002), we can describe the conflict between the municipality of Almada and the Fundo Margueira Capital as the clash of two conflicting "modernization projects" that relate themselves differently to stories of progress. According to Tsing, projects are "relatively coherent bundles of ideas and practices that are realized in particular times and places [...] Projects may articulate with each other, creating moments of fabled stability and power. They may also rub up against each other awkwardly, creating messiness and new possibilities" (Tsing 2002: 472). The modernization trajectory envisioned by Ricardo Nunes would have catapulted Almada out of its narrow local confines into the global arena. However, his vision failed and became "messy", precisely because it was not sufficiently re-embedded into local frameworks of meaning. Conversely, Mrs de Sousa, the political leaders, and the planners of Almada were able to seize new possibilities by skilfully and cleverly joining non-local and local objectives and options. Theirs is a glocal strategy which reinvents their community along the lines of a post-industrial modernity. However, for sure, the last chapter in the long saga of the Margueira has not been written yet.

Notes

1. Translation:
    Modern Almada [...]
    You possess force and beauty,
    And since the April came,
    You are the Portuguese town
    That has developed the most.
    Words by Maria dos Anjos Rodrigues Martins, Music by Mário Alexandre Pereira and Viana Caldeira Lopes. The text was published in the programme of the 2004 Marchas Populares by the Municipal Chamber of Almada.
2. However, the main population growth occurred before the revolution. In 1940, the population of Almada was only at 30,000, while in 1970, it had reached close to 110,000. In 2001, the census counted 159,550 inhabitants of Almada according to the Centro de Documentação do Museu da Cidade de Almada. The song's reference to the community's growth appears not to refer to a population increase, but to its economic and infrastructural development instead.
3. They were created in Lisbon in 1932 as a programme for a popular amusement park and grew into annual events that staged contests of folklore groups from the old Lisbon neighbourhoods. The Marchas gradually took the place of the traditional patron saints' feasts. In his historical analysis, Daniel Melo points out that these events were appropriated by the regime for its own political purposes from the 1950s onward (see Melo 2003). After the revolution, the Marchas Populares were discontinued. In 1979, the Lisbon Marchas were taken up again. Today, the Marchas that are being celebrated in many towns receive extensive media coverage and are aimed for the television audience.
4. The project is affiliated with the Institute of Cultural Anthropology and European Ethnology of Frankfurt University. It was funded by the German National Research Foundation DFG 2004-07. It was conducted by Eva Maria Blum as principal researcher under the direction of Gisela Welz. Preliminary research was done by Eva Maria Blum during 2000–04. Interviews were conducted with architects, city planners, politicians, representatives of the Margueira fund, civil servants in various functions and with residents in Almada itself as well as in neighbouring communities and the Greater Lisbon Area. Additionally, extensive participant observation at many public events and meetings was conducted, and a plethora of archival materials were analysed. Also, protagonists of the Portuguese discourse on urbanism and city planning, most of them well known architects and planners or social scientists, were interviewed. In Lisbon, the project cooperated closely with the Department of Anthropology at the ISCTE University and in particular with Professor Jorge Freitas Branco.
5. See Pina Cabral 1997, Leal 1999 and 2000.
6. As examples for this new trend in Portuguese anthropology, see for instance Bastos and Bastos 1999 and forthcoming, Cordeiro et al. 2003, Malheiros 2000 and 2002, Mapril 2002, Sanches 2006, and Silvano 2002.
7. Another problem associated with suburbanization in Portugal is the fact that most buildings outside of city limits have been constructed illegally without building permits. This also holds true for many cases of middle-class suburban developments.
8. For an overview and a critical assessment, see Welz 2004.
9. Needless to say, in Lisbon like anywhere else in the period before 9/11, to speak of the towers of Manhattan merely meant a reference to spectacularly high buildings, buildings that would seem out of place in other cities.
10. Interestingly enough, this argument completely disregarded the fact that the southern shoreline of the Tagus since the beginning of the twentieth century had been disfigured by industrial installations of various kinds.
11. The influential Portuguese industrialist family Mello was one of the partners in the company CUF that founded the Lisnave shipyards. Lisnave had very early on started to expand internationally, first with the construction of dry docks in Bahrain in 1977.
12. After the revolution, industrial companies and in

particular huge landholdings of the aristocracy, were brought under state control. Later, these measures were retracted. In addition, state-owned enterprises started to become privatised in the 1980s. See Freire 2000. For an ethnographic account of the post-revolutionary restructuring of Portuguese agriculture, see Dracklé 1991.
13 Since then, the Communist Party has somewhat changed its stance. The Communist Party-dominated municipal government of Almada, for one, is strongly advocating European integration today.
14 Interview Ricardo Nunes conducted on March 6, 2001.
15 Interview Ricardo Nunes conducted on March 6, 2001.
16 During the high times of the shipyard, there were up to 10,000 workers employed on the site.
17 From an article in *Construção Limitada* of Sept. 1, 1999, published on the website www.civilium.net/infocil/manhattan.shtml, accessed on Jan. 3, 2005.
18 *Expresso* November 25, 2000; www.ulissul.com, accessed December 2005.
19 *Expresso* May 19, 2001.
20 Interview Ricardo Nunes conducted on March 6, 2001
21 See articles in newspapers such as *Expresso* on Feb. 12, 2005, and *Jornal das Letras*, March 15, 2005.
22 Nunes found that three huge billboards that the Fundo had placed at strategic points within the town of Almada were removed by the municipality within a day. Nunes subsequently accused the municipal government of censorship in public.
23 This is a frequent criticism voiced by political opponents to the Communist Party in Portugal that – unlike its Italian sister party, for instance – has never officially distanced itself from Stalinism.
24 *Expresso* April 24, 1999.
25 For a more detailed analysis, see Ferreira & Indovina 1999.
26 In a letter to the mayoral office of Almada, sent early in 2002, he announced that he stepped down from his position of the board of the real estate fund: "I take this opportunity to praise her Excellency for the honour and pleasure to have had you as my most faithful enemy for all these years. I want to emphasize the contrast between the iron determination of those who opposed me and the muddy cleverness of those who should have defended me." Original e-mail received from Ricardo Nunes on Feb. 8, 2002.
27 For more information on the implementation of the strategy for citizens' participation within the framework of the Frente Ribeirinha Nascente project of the municipality of Almada, see Blum 2007.
28 Meanwhile, the plan has been published as an attractive coffee-table book in Portuguese and English with many photographs. See Câmara Municipal de Almada 2006.
29 In the collective memory of Almada residents, "bathing at the Margueira beach" is an important topic which was reactivated in the discussions of the new project of the Cidade de Agua. See Blum forthcoming.
30 Almada is one of 27 Portuguese municipalities that are developing a local Agenda 21, and also belongs to the network of European municipalities that have signed the Charta of Aalborg, committing themselves to sustainable development.

References

Appadurai, Arjun 1996: *Modernity at Large. Cultural Dimensions of Globalization*. Minneapolis, London: University of Minnesota Press.

Argyrou, Vassos 1996: *Tradition and Modernity in the Mediterranean: The Wedding as Symbolic Struggle*. Cambridge: Cambridge University Press.

Barreto, António (ed.) 2000: *A Situação Social em Portugal, 1960–1999*. Lisboa: Imprensa de Ciências Sociais.

Bastos, José Gabriel Pereira & Susana Pereira Bastos 1999: *Portugal multicultural. Situação e estratégias identitárias das minorias étnicas*. Lisboa: Fim de Século.

Bastos, José Gabriel Pereira, J. Dahinden, P. Goís & C. Westin (eds.) forthcoming: *Identity Processes and Strategies in Multiethnic Europe*. Amsterdam: Amsterdam University Press.

Berg, Per Olof, Anders Linde-Laursen & Orvar Löfgren (eds.) 2000: *Invoking a Transnational Metropolis. The Making of the Öresund Region*. Lund: Studentlitteratur.

Blum, Eva Maria 2007: Planungskulturen im Konflikt: Stadtumbau im Großraum Lissabon. *Zeitschrift für Volkskunde*. Vol. 103 No. I, 39-63.

Blum, Eva Maria forthcoming: Überbaute Erinnerungen. Die Neuverhandlung von Kultur, Erbe und Geschichte im Verlauf eines Stadtumbauprojektes im Großraum Lissabon. Submitted to *Schweizerisches Archiv für Volkskunde*.

Bouquet, Mary (ed.) 1999: Academic Anthropology and the Museum: Back to the Future. In: *Focaal* 34.

Branco, Jorge Freitas 1982: Aspekte der ethnologischen Forschung in Portugal: Quellen, Vorläufer, Tendenzen. In: T. Hauschild & H. Nixdorff (eds.), *Europäische Ethnologie. Theorie- und Methodendiskussion aus ethnologischer und volkskundlicher Sicht*. Berlin: Dietrich Reimer Verlag, 129–136.

Câmara Municipal de Almada 2006: *Almada Nascente. Estudo de caracterização ambiental, geológica e geotécnica e plano de urbanização da frente ribeirinha nascente da Cidade de Almada. Eastern Almada – Environmental, Geotechnical and Geological Study and Urban Masterplan of the Eastern Almada Riverfront*, Vol. 1. Atkins, Santa-Rita Arquitectos, Richard Rogers Partnership.

Clifford, James & George Marcus 1986: *Writing Culture. The Poetics and Politics of Ethnography*. Berkeley: University of

California Press.
Cordeiro, Graça Indias, Luís Vicente Batista & Antonio Firmino da Costa (eds.) 2003: *Etnografias urbanas*. Oeiras: Celta Editora.
Draclé, Dorle 1991: *Macht und Ohnmacht. Der Kampf um die Agrarreform im Alentejo. Eine diskursanalytische Untersuchung zur Strukturierung von Machtbeziehungen am Beispiel einer südportugiesischen Kooperative*. Göttingen: Edition Re.
El-Shawan Castelo-Branco, Salwa & Jorge Freitas Branco (eds.) 2003: *Vozes de Povo. A Folclorização em Portugal*. Oeiras: Celta Editora.
Ferreira, Vítor Matias & Francesco Indovina (eds.) 1999: *A cidade da Expo*. Lisbon: Editorial Bizâncio.
Freire, João 2000: Companies and Organisations: Change and Modernisation. In: J.M. Leite Viegas & A. F. da Costa (eds.), *Crossroads to Modernity. Contemporary Portuguese Society*. Oeiras: Celta, 261–278.
Frykman, Jonas & Orvar Löfgren 1987: *Culture Builders: A Historical Anthropology of Middle-Class Life*. New Brunswick: Rutgers University Press.
Geertz, Clifford 1995: *After the Fact. Two Countries, Four Decades, One Anthropologist*. Cambridge, London: Harvard University Press.
Hannerz, Ulf 1996. The Glocal Ecumene as a Landscape of Modernity. In: *Transnational Connections. Culture, People, Places*. London, New York: Routledge, 44–55.
Herzfeld, Michael 1992: *The Social Production of Indifference. Exploring the Symbolic Roots of Western Bureaucracy*. Chicago, London: University of Chicago Press.
Holston, James 1989: *The Modernist City: An Anthropological Critique of Brasilia*. Chicago: University of Chicago Press.
Kahn, Joel S. 2001: Anthropology and Modernity. *Current Anthropology* 42:5, 651–664.
Leal, João 1999: The History of Portuguese Anthropology http://anthropology.uchicago.edu/about/han/leal.thm.
Leal, João 2000: *Etnografias Portuguesas (1870–1970). Cultura Popular e identidade nacional*. Lisboa: Publicações Dom Quixote.
Lourenço, Eduardo 1997: *Portugal – Europa. Mythos und Melancholie. Essays*. Frankfurt am Main: Verlag Theo Ferrer de Mesquita.
Machado, Fernando Luís & António Firmino da Costa 2000: An Incomplete Modernity. In: J.M. Leite Viegas & A. F. da Costa (eds.), *Crossroads to Modernity. Contemporary Portuguese Society*. Oeiras: Celta, 15–40.
Malheiros, Jorge Macaísta 2000: Urban Restructuring, Immigration and the Generation of Marginalized Spaces in the Lisbon Region. In: R. King, G. Lazarides & C. Tsardanides (eds.), *Eldorado or Fortress? Migration in Southern Europe*. London: Routledge, 207–231.
Malheiros, Jorge Macaísta et al. (eds.) 2002: *Immigration and Place in Mediterranean Metropolises*. Lisbon: Luso-American Foundation & Metropolis Portugal.

Mapril, José 2002: Transnational Jade Formations: the Translocal Practices of Chinese Immigrants in a Lisbon Innercity Neighbourhood. In: F. Eckardt (ed.), *Consumption and the Post-Industrial City. The European City in Transition*. Frankfurt, New York: Peter Lang Publishers.
Marcus, George E. & Michael M.J. Fischer 1986: *Anthropology as Cultural Critique. An Experimental Moment in the Human Sciences*. Chicago: University of Chicago Press.
Melo, Daniel 2003: As Marchas Populares: a encenação da cidade de Lisboa. In: S. El-Shawan Castelo-Branco & J. Freitas Branco (eds.), *Vozes de Povo. A Folclorização em Portugal*. Oeiras: Celta, 307–322.
Ong, Aihwa 1999: *Flexible Citizenship: The Cultural Logics of Transnationality*. Durham, London: Duke University Press.
Ong, Aihwa 2001: Modernity: Anthropological Aspects. In: *International Encyclopedia of the Social and Behavioral Sciences*. Amsterdam: Elsevier, 9944–9949.
Pina Cabral, João 1997: Breves Considerações sobre o Estado da Antropologia em Portugal. *Antropologia Portuguesa*, Vol. 7, 29–36.
Rabinow, Paul 1989: *French Modern. Norms and Forms of the Social Environment* Cambridge: MIT Press.
Robertson, Roland 1998: Glokalisierung: Homogenität und Heterogenität in Raum und Zeit. In: Ulrich Beck (ed.), *Perspektiven der Weltgesellschaft*. Frankfurt/M.: Suhrkamp, 192–200.
Rodenstein, Marianne 2006: Globalisierung und ihre visuelle Repräsentation in europäischen Städten durch Hochhäuser. In: M. Faßler & C. Terkowsky (eds.), *Urban Fictions. Die Zukunft des Städtischen*. München: Wilhelm Fink Verlag, 83–100.
Sanches, Manuela Ribeiro (ed.) 2006: *Portugal não é um país pequeno – contar o "império na pós-colonialidade"*. Lissabon: Livros Cotovia.
Silvano, Filomena 2002: José e Jacinta nem sempre vivem nos mesmos lugares: reflexões em torno de uma etnografia multi-situada. In: J. G. P. Bastos (ed.), Antropologia dos processos identitários (número temático), *Ethnologia* (ns), nos 12–14. Lisboa: Fim de Seculo, 53–79.
Tsing, Anna 2002: The Global Situation. In: J. X. Inda & R. Rosaldo (eds.), *The Anthropology of Globalization. A Reader*. Malden MA, Oxford UK: Blackwell, 453–486.
Viegas, José Manuel Leite & António Firmino da Costa 2000: Introduction. Overlapping Processes of Social Change. In: J.M. Leite Viegas & A. F. da Costa (eds.), *Crossroads to Modernity. Contemporary Portuguese Society*. Oeiras: Celta, 1–14.
Welz, Gisela 2004: Transnational Cultures and Multiple Modernities. Anthropology's Encounter with Globalization. In: Günter H. Lenz, Gesa Mackenthun & Holger Rossow (eds.), 'Between Worlds': the Legacy of Edward Said. *ZAA Quarterly*, Vol. 52 (4): 409–422.

Gisela Welz is professor of Cultural Anthropology and European Ethnology at Frankfurt University. Her most recent publication is *Divided Cyprus. Modernity, History, and an Island in Conflict* (edited together with Yiannis Papadakis and Nicos Peristianis 2006). She cooperated with Eva Maria Blum on the research project Urbanization as a Cultural Project: Urban Renewal in Greater Lisbon 2004–06.
(G.Welz@em.uni-frankfurt.de,
http://www.uni-frankfurt.de/fb/fb09/kulturanthro/staff/welz_home.html)

Eva Maria Blum is teaching at the Institute of Cultural Anthropology and European Ethnology of Frankfurt University and works with the Municipal Office for Multicultural Affairs of the City of Frankfurt. In 1991, she published a book on corporate culture and industrial restructuring of a Frankfurt neighbourhood in German *Kultur, Konzern, Konsens. Die Hoechst AG und der Frankfurter Stadtteil Höchst*. She conducted fieldwork in the research project Urbanization as a Cultural Project: Urban Renewal in Greater Lisbon 2004–06 as principal researcher.
(e.m.blum@t-online.de,
http://www.uni-frankfurt.de/fb/fb09/kulturanthro/research.html)

THE OUTSIDER'S GAZE AS PART OF THE METHODOLOGICAL TOOLKIT?
Reflections on the Research Project the "Musikantenstadl"

Gebhard Fartacek

Under the slogan "you research us", a Turkish sociologist and a Romanian art philosopher were invited by the Austrian Academy of Sciences to get to the bottom of the success of the musical television event "Der Musikantenstadl". The article discusses the experiences with the concept of the "outsider's gaze" from the point of view of the (native) project coordinator. The first section discusses the classic principle of social anthropological field research: "We research you". The author reflects on his own field research practice in the Middle East where being an outsider played an important role with regard to the reliability and quality of the investigation results. The second section summarizes the "conscious exotisation" through an outsider's perspective as applied in the research project on the Musikantenstadl.

Keywords: methodology, Musikantenstadl, folk music, Austria, Syria

Investigating the Musikantenstadl from an Outsider's Perspective

What is the *Musikantenstadl*? This phenomenon showcasing popular Alpine culture is quite familiar to most people in the German-speaking countries of Europe. But even without ever seeing it, most readers are likely to have an idea what it is about.

First, there is the successful television production from Austrian Television (ORF) with Karl Moik, the originator, creator, and presenter of this program, which has been broadcast at more or less monthly intervals since 1981. Most German speaking television viewers (including those who do not watch the program) have heard of the Musikantenstadl. It was originally shown on a Thursday evening, but today Stadl fans can make themselves comfortable in front of the television at peak viewing time and watch the *Volksmusik* show at 8.15 p.m. on a Saturday evening, entranced by Karl Moik's presentation.[1] Volksmusik here is not the same as folk music; it is a mixed program with both popular and traditional songs. The shows are mainly live, direct broadcasts from the hall, tent, or similar type of venue in which the Musikantenstadl takes place before an audience.

Second, the Musikantenstadl is also a live show that is held in more or less well-known towns and villages, mainly in German-speaking regions. This is the form favoured by the die-hard fans who travel to the various event locations. For these locations, the organization of a Musikantenstadl is an effective marketing tool and also a boost to tourism, not just for the duration of the event. For the fans, the live settings hold the chance to see their favorite musicians, to see the event first hand – yes, and maybe even to be filmed by the camera and appear, however briefly "on television". A special feature of this Volksmusik program is the *Auslandsstadl* (the Stadl abroad) It was established as a kind of cultural exchange and as an opportunity for fans of the program to travel abroad with the fan club. Travel agencies also offer longer trips with the "Stadl family", for example, "Karl Moik and the Sea", a seven-day themed cruise on the Baltic Sea including "Musikantenstadl en route" each day.

Third, the Musikantenstadl is also available in the form of the newspaper *Stadlpost*, published ten times a year, providing the fans with all kinds of background information. If you want to know how Volksmusik star Hansi Hinterseer spends Christmas and what kind of snugness is most important for him at this time of year, this is the place to get informed. The *Stadlpost* is now also available on the Internet under the address http://www.stadlpost.at, and includes an online forum with active discussions on topics affecting the Stadl world.

Fourth, the *Musikantenstadl*© is trademarked. From Stadl bread to Stadl wine, there are countless Stadl products and they all use a standardized labeling, sometimes including a portrait of Karl Moiks. These Stadl products have their price, but they are exclusive and of good quality.

And finally, fifth, the Musikantenstadl is a bit like the Vienna Boys' Choir, Lipizzaner horses, and the traditional chocolates *Mozartkugeln* (cf. Luger 1990: 72–96): It is a synonym for Austrian culture abroad, whereby the Austria represented by the Musikantenstadl is purportedly rural, down-to-earth, and natural instead of urban and elitist. It is "Austria's business card for the world", as the executive producer of the Musikantenstadl, Ursula Stiedl of ORF, once said. It is something that the Alpine republic identifies with, like a collective identity marker – to the joy of those who love it and the horror of those who hate it. Musikantenstadl is not just a keyword hiding many different associations; it is a *piece of popular culture*, constructed out of the confluence of the mass-medium television, the twentieth century Volksmusik recording industry and nostalgia for a *Volk* construct contained within this repertoire. And it has been highly disputed since the start of its existence.

It is in this context – the Musikantenstadl as a synonym for Alpine popular culture, as an Austrian business card, and as a disputed piece of culture – that the Musikantenstadl was chosen as a site for cultural research. From July 2004 to December 2006 a project was launched at the Austrian Academy of Sciences (ÖAW: Social Anthropology Unit) with the title *Alpine Populärkultur im fremden Blick: Der Musikantenstadl im Lichte der Wissenschaften [Alpine popular culture seen through the eyes of a stranger: The Musikantenstadl from a research perspective].*[2] The project was based on examining, through outsiders' eyes, the public spectacle Musikantenstadl with its roots in multiply mediated Alpine culture. It has become more common in cultural and social anthropology that in addition to the dominant "we study you" situation, a "we study ourselves" (as perhaps more customary in European Ethnology) or "you study yourself" option is added. In the project discussed here, the variant "you study us" was central, resulting in a methodological paradigm change. Researchers with an outsider's view from Romania (Mădălina Diaconu) and Turkey (Zeynep Baraz) were included for the deliberate "exotisation" of the perspective on the Stadl.

In the conception of the research project, it was assumed that a view from outside would highlight other and new perspectives, insights, and interpretations that might exceed those of Austrian researchers encumbered by implicit understandings and a native cultural identity (see the discussion in Altheide 1996: 2). It is this implicitness of culture that makes it difficult to recognize special features and to differentiate these from the "unimportant" or less marked aspects within one's own cultural environment. Given the Musikantenstadls high visibility as a mass mediated event, with a tradition of more than twenty years, made this methodological option all the more important. For Austrians it is almost impossible to view the Stadl separately from an equally visible public discourse on the aesthetics and politics encoded in the repertoire, the performers and staging typical of any given Stadl evening.

My research-based interest in social science methodology in general and in particular the development of new ethnological methods of data collection formed the main link to this research project. In autumn 2004 when I was invited to take on the coordination of the research project, I had mixed feelings: On the one hand, the task did not really seem to fit with my academic background because my regional area of expertise was the ethnography of the Arabian peninsula. By this point, I had already spent more than two years of my life carrying out ethnological field research in the Middle East. In the course of this, I made acquaintance with popular religious pilgrimages, local conceptions of spirits and demons, with taboos and rituals and their significance for religious and daily actions. So it was a quite different situation that I should suddenly find myself dealing with the Musikantenstadl, a media event within my own culture. On the other hand, I saw in my biography diverse situations in which I had been confronted with elements of Alpine popular culture that had preoccupied me, both emotionally and mentally. And then there was also the opportunity for me as a social anthropologist to confront completely new areas of research. In the end, the deciding factor for accepting the offer was the long-held wish to cooperate with others in research projects instead of being a "lone ranger".

The experiences gathered in the areas of project organization and interdisciplinarity and their linkage to the methodological inclusion of the "outsider's gaze" are the subject of this article. Based on my work in the Middle East, I will first focus on dimensions of being an outsider inherent in ethnographic practice (Gingrich 2006a: 25). I will begin with reflections on my own field research practice in which my non-native status of the researcher played an important role – with regard to the concrete research options and the reliability and quality of research results (cf. Steinke 2003: 319–331). From there I will move to the research project *Alpine popular culture seen through the eyes of a stranger* in which the principle of the outsider's view was defined as a central part of the methodological inventory. Through an account of my experiences as a project coordinator responsible for content as well as administrative issues, this article[3] will reflect on the lessons gathered through the "method" of the outsider's gaze (in the sense of "you study us"). Advantages as well as difficulties and dangers connected to this approach will be discussed. The paper then proceeds to a theoretical conceptualization of this distancing and examines the possibility to operationalize it as part of the methodological toolkit. Finally, the results of the investigation into the Musikantenstadl phenomenon[4] will be discussed along with an account of the enormously high media reception of this research project.

Ethnological Field Research in the Middle East

Ethnography is a methodological core competence of cultural and social anthropology. Basically, ethnography consists of extended local observation in the actors' community. The participant observers or ethnographers usually bring a certain prior understanding "from without" and participate in the events to be investigated as "professional strangers". This type of external gaze is detailed and exact, because the process as a whole focuses on the trivialities of everyday life as seen through the eyes of external novices who often tend to see the forest instead of the individual trees (Gingrich 2006a: 25).

Continuing this metaphor – grasping the forest by combining the individual trees – within the framework of my own field research practice, I would add that the "professional stranger" (cf. Agar 1980) tends to have fewer prejudices against the individual trees and considers them generally with less bias than do many locals. In an unfamiliar situation, it is easier to be cosmopolitan and more impartial. It is a central ethnological principle to be open for everything and to take each cultural phenomenon seriously, even if it appears irrelevant at first, because everything can be significant in seeking coherent explanations. In the field, the ethnographer does well to withhold his own value judgments. I do not go into the field as a missionary who tries to convert. Rather, I seek to understand *how* people think and in which contexts and in which "necessary relationships" (Oppitz 1993) this occurs. To be at home in the research context is thus a bit different: At home I feel compelled to debate the culture, to criticize and denounce social and political conditions. I might like to attract people to my ideas – and as I see it, at home there is also a certain obligation to keep up a position of the responsible citizen; striving for a society based on equality and not lapsing into apolitical behavior that would accept everything as it is.

When working in the Middle East, however, particular local cultural norms and values will hold a special significance: As a polite person, I will respect the opinions of others. If someone makes a statement, I ought to agree or make no comment if I really do not agree. It is not prudent to get into an argument straight away with the other party. Living empathy is easier in such situations than at home. "Empathy" is the ability to put oneself in another's position. There is a difference between cognitive and affective aspects of empathy, the former concerns the ability to understand the "intellectual world" of another person, the latter comprises the feelings and emotions of another person. My working assumption is that mustering empathy and the attendant understanding of the feelings of others is particularly difficult within a context roughly labeled as "home" in the sense of the socio-political field of public, national interaction – a context, in short, within which the Musikantenstadl phenomenon is situated. To illustrate what is meant by this, I would like to include an example from my own ethnographic research.

Between 1997 and 2001 I was dealing extensively with local shrines in the peripheral areas of the modern-day Arabian Republic of Syria (Fartacek 2003a). Always situated in unusual locations such as mountain peaks, strange trees or holy wells, in caves and rocky crevices, these holy shrines are connected to ancient myths and legends and linked to mythological persons. In pre-Islamic times, these places were untouchable refuges and sanctuaries for asylum seekers who were under "divine protection". Although customary law has lost its meaning since then, local shrines are still places for discovering the truth and seek rehabilitation and reconciliation. Interestingly, the places of pilgrimage in the Syrian border area are often visited equally by members of different ethnic and religious groups. As an ethnological field researcher, I documented these holy places and carried out interviews with pilgrims from very different backgrounds. Most of my conversational partners were deeply religious individuals. Through conversations, I tried to find out *how* my interview partners thought and which views of the world were behind their indexical everyday language expressions. In the course of the research process, I developed great empathy and a kind of "understanding" for the views and explanation models of my interview partners. I experienced a real fascination for these popular religious conceptions and was subsequently keen to emphasize the positive aspects of these local belief systems in lectures and discussions. To subject my own behavior during the research process to a methodological-critical reflection and, if necessary, to adapt it, I maintained a research diary (cf. Flick 1995: 191). In the course of the research, it became obvious that my enthusiasm for the popular religious pilgrimages was to a large extent linked to the location and the research situation and that I would probably have had a completely different approach to this subject in "my homeland" of Austria where there certainly also are pilgrimage sites to be found. I do not remember whether it had ever occurred to me to investigate the cognitive world of pilgrims in Austria or even to make a pilgrimage to the famous holy site of Mariazell. To be honest, I feel somewhat startled about people who carry out pilgrimages there. The Cult of the Virgin Mary and the organized bus trips from other European countries seem suspect to me. It would not have occurred to me to connect the places of pilgrimage along the Syrian borders with the Austrian Mariazell – the clientele is too different, as is the social function of pilgrimage and the worldviews through which the sites are classified as holy. While comparative research on these phenomena might indeed be productive, I am left with the recognition that in one's home context, one's research tolerance is different than in a foreign land. This estrangement facilitates, I would argue, greater impartiality and a higher degree of empathy. Hence, the status as "professional stranger" in ethnographic field research offers a methodological potential which we were able to use successfully in the project *Alpine popular culture seen through the eyes of a stranger.*

It is not only the ethnologist who usually confronts

conversation partners as a "professional stranger". The ethnologist, in turn, will normally be shown more tolerance by the host group, as his behavior is judged less strictly. In particular in the Middle East, where relational alliances play a major role, the outsider is viewed as impartial by the locals, even if he is awarded the status of the guest family when there is doubt. The stranger must be helped and if he behaves "incorrectly", more tolerant procedures are applied, he is forgiven more easily, and the most naïve questions are not taken badly – for he is interested in something but does not know exactly what (cf. Fartacek 2003b). This can be illustrated with my effort to collect ethnographic data on the conception of the blessing power of God, the *baraka*.

If one asks a pilgrim in the Middle East for reasons for visiting local shrines, one repeatedly hears the "simple" answer: *min shan al-baraka!* Because of the *baraka*. For a researcher from Syria where "every child knows what baraka is", it would be difficult to expand the answer. The interested foreigner from Austria, however, who still has problems with the language, will be entitled to ask for further explanations. This foreigner can also ask such naïve questions and one will patiently explain to him what baraka is – a blessing power that is originally given by God and manifesting itself in particular places, objects, and persons. The baraka can be transferred from these carriers to "normal" people by carrying out specific rituals. Baraka improves both the material and spiritual situation of the people. It is a therapy for illness or infertility, and it offers protection from demonic influences, black magic and the effect of the evil eye. It is also helpful in the resolution of personal or collective problems.

I think that the "professional stranger" can in fact learn more here than a person accepted as a local. In the best case, such a question would be considered naïve, in the worst case (which can occur in particular if the person inquiring is a Syrian who belongs to a different ethnic-religious group), a question of this nature could be interpreted as an attack on one's own beliefs.

It is important to note in this context that in colloquial Arabian language use, existing norms and values are usually formulated as descriptive rather than normative expressions. Desired perceptions, for example, "it is important to be tolerant in questions of religion" are formulated as actual states, such as, "with us, there are no difficulties and followers of all religious communities make pilgrimages to this shrine". This situation must also be taken into account when formulating questions or interpreting the answers in ethnographic data collection (Fartacek 2003a: 202). To master the dialectally "restricted" language code plays a key role in the present context as, in contrast to "elaborate" literary language, it brings emotion to the expression.

This "ask what and how locals could not ask"[5] is particularly relevant if the research process is conceived as a hypothesis-generating dialogue with the interview partners in the sense of Grounded Theory (Strauss 1991). The invitation to further explanation arises "naturally" in such interview situations. In general the conversation partners make an effort to explain everything to the "professional stranger" – and these explanations enable the researcher to interpret and obtain additional understanding, which usually exceeds what the locals (can) see themselves in an everyday context or what – if asked by a "native" – they might not wish to divulge.

From an epistemological perspective, the unfamiliarity of the researcher plays a particularly important role for creating structural coherences. In the Middle East, this understanding is equivalent to an emic perspective. In the course of my ethnographic field research a parable was told to me many times, which originally comes from the tradition of sufism; it makes different viewpoints the subject of discussion. These can be outlined through the metaphor inside/secular versus outside/sacred (Fartacek 2003a: 155).

According to the story, there are basically two different types of viewpoints: the view of the worm on one side and the view of the bird on the other. According to the tradition, the worm sees the things lying before him, very large and clear – however, he cannot recognize what is hiding behind them. This is the view of the "normal" person in society. In contrast, the bird comes from unfamiliar surroundings, looks down on the world from above, and sees everything in context. He recognizes what is hidden behind the individual objects that are before him. He can see what, how, and where things are connected and he can create reciprocal relationships between the things for he has a multi-dimensional or complete view. The view of the bird is the view of the outsider, and also the view of a pilgrim, who at his place of pilgrimage, at the peak of the holy mountain – also metaphorically speaking – lets his gaze run over the secular world below (cf. Baumann 2002: 163–187).

The view of the outsider (or the person who is not immersed in the everyday world) is also confirmed here as being able to recognize and interpret the coherences and reciprocal relationships of everyday life. Thus this view is not so distant from that which Andre Gingrich addressed with the metaphor "coming from outside, you see the forest better than the individual trees", referring to "the ethnographic, external gaze". Unfamiliarity can become the key to grasping an emic perspective – in particular if it concerns the formation of structural coherences and "necessary relationships" (Oppitz 1993).

The Stranger's Gaze in Action

The theoretical and methodological conception of the Musikantenstadl project sought to utilize the "external gaze" of non-native researchers as an intrinsic component of the investigation. With the project completed and published it is possible to evaluate the effectiveness of this approach. Were the non-native researchers actually more impartial in their approach than Austrian ethnologists could have been? Are there indicators to measure whether non-native researchers achieved quantitatively and qualitatively different results? Was the approach of asking naïve questions – or, as Mādālina Diaconu summarized it critically, to have a "jester's licence" (2006: 228) – productive? And in particular: did the design actually allow a "view from above" that enabled a better recognition of coherences? I will try to provide some answers to these questions below.

From February 2005 to January 2006[6] – during the phase of intensive data collection – project group meetings were held approximately every 14 days. The overriding aim of these group meetings was to encourage dialog between the members of the project group and to discuss the common points as well as differences between the individual scholarly approaches on the one hand, and, on the other hand, to discuss the external (represented by the foreign project team members) and internal perspectives (represented by the Austrian project team members). In addition, we addressed upcoming practical questions of data collection and data interpretation and tried to come to a basic consensus in the explanation of central concepts, such as "identity" or "(popular) culture" as used within the different research settings as well as the different disciplines involved. Evidence for the outsider's gaze not just in fieldwork but also in these team meetings emerge in Mādālina Diaconu's reflections. She writes about her efforts to render the Musikantenstadl less "demonic", removing it from the hotly and critically rejected space it held in aspects of the Austrian public discourse. She noted horrified cries of many of her interview partners who could not fathom seeing the program in a harmless, "just-so" fashion – a stance she also found represented among the native members of our team during informal conversational situations during or outside of the team meetings. The native–non-native dynamic thus was a productive component in the field as much as in the analytic group settings, and continually pointed out to me as coordinator the necessity to examine my own, far from latent, sentiments about our object of research.

Whether scholar or sausage stand owner – I suspect there are hardly any Austrians who are indifferent to the Musikantenstadl phenomenon. In this context – working with a nationally known media event – the "external gaze" was advantageous. Examining the data assembled, it is obvious that Mādālina Diaconu and Zeynep Baraz were much more impartial than I or likely most other native researchers could have been. Diaconu and Baraz did participant observation on the stage set during the live recordings, interviewed Karl Moik and other individuals involved in the production; they interviewed individuals who held definite opinions about the Stadl and visited small town festivals and musical events where popular music similar to the Stadl-repertoire was performed. Unperturbed by public valuation of musical taste traditions and their social, political and regional associations in Austria, they could document behaviors, elicit narratives and commentaries without interference from their own aesthetic socialization.

As project coordinator I was in turn grateful to be removed from such ethnographic immediacy. My emotional stance toward the Musikantenstadl had always been negative. I grew up in the country side of Upper Austria, most of my relatives live in the countryside of Salzburg and my leisure activities as well as my West-Austrian roots continue to draw me to the mountains. From a young age I was thus confronted by a mass-mediated *Volkskultur*, of which some elements are indeed reappropriated in rural settings. As a city dweller, preferring urban heterogeneity, the distance from an at once real and staged "folk scene" has grown, and encountering it brings about a sense of being unable to "defend myself". My association with the Musikantenstadl was and remains profoundly shaped by these biographical components – which I share with many other Austrians; the Stadl embodies "sociability", if not quite "folkish sociability", a small inn environment that smacks of beer table politics, a bit of camaraderie, a bit of Carinthian sentimentality, and a bit of the feel of a Sudeten-German voluntary association.[7] Added to all of this are the parameters of a live television show, applause on demand, public acclaim, and an odd enthusiasm. Despite the intensive engagement with the phenomenon as coordinator of the Stadl project it is hard to suppress the negative associations inherent for me with the Stadl and similar phenomena which I tend to avoid at all costs.

The more open I was when confronted with the pilgrims in Syria, the more prejudiced I might have turned as an investigator of the Musikantenstadl. The interest in the subject and the understanding of interview partners, in their sensitivities and emotions, might have hindered the withholding of my value judgments: This ethnographic stance would have been hard to muster and likely not have been convincing to many interview partners. Without doubt many interview partners would have sensed my inner ambiguity and might have closed up or even sought to get me to reveal my own views.

The question of how I might have dealt with facing comparable mass mediated phenomena in the local popular culture of the Middle East arises. Would I have struggled with my prejudices in similar ways? On the basis of my Syrian research experience I would assume the case to be quite different and the Stadl project with its two non-native researchers would seem to confirm this stance. Lack of familiarity is a positive condition for field research, especially so for grasping the cultural context of a media event. It enables the interview partners to provide more differentiated explanations and more authentic explorations. The researchers in turn can approach the research site and its context from a distance, free of the stress the same event brings for the native scholar. This became evident in many commentaries by Baraz and Diaconu as they prepared for the fieldwork. "What is up with them (the Austrians)?" they would ask, "Why are they so hysterical?" "The Musikantenstadl is not that unusual and could be found anywhere in the world", noted Baraz, and Diaconu maintained that the demonization of the program common among a sizable segment of the interviewees should be abandoned and the understanding of the phenomenon should, instead, be nurtured.

Both Baraz and Diaconu brought in addition to an "external gaze" also the knowledge and perspectives of additional disciplinary specializations, namely sociology and philosophy. Diaconu's remarks on the aesthetics of the Musikantenstadl (2006: 155–228) in particular led me to ask whether my prejudices could be assuaged through the addition of specialized knowledge – from aesthetics, philosophy, and media studies. "Understanding" could be accrued through assembling an outsider's perspectives in multiple senses of the term. Appropriate specialized knowledge further increased the emotional distance to the Musikantenstadl and related phenomena of Alpine popular culture. At the same time, this knowledge contributed a beneficial component in the meetings with the interview partners; it furthered the non-judgmental atmosphere and improved the understanding between researcher and researched. The Stadl project was thus not just improved, but perhaps made possible in the first place through the inclusion of a both ethnographically and disciplinarily "external gaze": Data collection, interpretation, and analysis profited from the greater impartiality warranted through this methodological choice.

Ethnographic work in the Middle East appears to differ from that in Austria on one fundamental point: the interested foreigner was received more warmly in the Middle East than here at home. I still shudder when I remember Zeynep Baraz' descriptions of the village festival in Hollabrunn that she participated in as part of the research (Baraz 2006: 131ff). Her commentaries provide a vivid impression of how one is treated as an "inquisitive Turk" in the Alpine republic. Although the gathering was probably not composed of stereotypical right-wing extremists, people nonetheless made it quite clear to the researcher from abroad that she had no business being there. Initial contact is, as most ethnographers will know, not always smooth, but if one is greeted at a village festivity with comments on how one may not simply sit at any table, one needs a very thick skin. Similarly, the rejection letter from the management of the Viennese Senior Citizen Society reproduced by Mādālina Diaconu (2006: 156) shows that the process of data collection was not always easy for the researchers. In response to her friendly request of whether she could visit a Sunday club in connection with our research project, she received the answer that there was no interest in helping her if there was not to be any remuneration, and that she ought to "use a professional institute for an individual sample composition". Both incidents raise the question of how the two researchers were perceived – as foreigners or migrants. It is furthermore likely that judgments concerning the place of origin of non-native researchers in this "you study us" modality of research prove to be highly significant and could constitute a theme of reflection on the research findings.[8]

Nonetheless, the research design featuring non-native researchers yielded the ethnographic dimensions we had hoped for: Because the researchers were seen as outsiders, their questions about the Musikantenstadl seemed less absurd to the conversation partners. Zeynep Baraz and Mādālina Diaconu were thus told "more". They were also able to ask "naïve" questions – questions that it would not befit an Austrian to ask. Possibly, the fact that the researchers were outsiders was also a reason why Austrian television (the ORF) was so benevolent and supportive from the start. Fears that the Musikantenstadl might have been critically exposed would have been completely understandable, but nothing of the sort was presented to us.[9]

Entry into the field and contact with main protagonists particularly on the set was smoothed through a further project team member, the Viennese economist Wolfgang Fellner. His social competence paved the way to the decision makers at ORF and was also instrumental in securing the open interview with the program's host, Karl Moik. The combination of foreign and native participants in the project as a whole is thus highly recommended. In addition to establishing contacts, participation by natives in the analysis of data is relevant as a source of synergy and, more pragmatically, to clarify linguistic and paralinguistic elements which may benefit from a native understanding. This was particularly relevant in our project, as we realized when working through fieldwork materials in team sessions. Both foreign researchers speak excellent German. They did, however, have problems understanding some of the jokes and innuendos that form a part of Karl Moik's Musikantenstadl performance. Significantly, Zeynep Baraz and Mādālina Diaconu rarely chose to focus on gender relations in their contributions on the Musikantenstadl (cf. Baraz 2006: 119–154; Diaconu 2006: 155–227; Baraz & Diaconu 2006: 229–248) – which again may be attributable to their non-native status. In project discussions or when watching the recordings of the Stadl together, I sometimes had the impression that the non-Austrian researchers did not catch the sexist double standards of some expressions and consequently did not really comprehend why so many interview partners described the presenter Karl Moik as "bawdy".

Such differences in registering Stadl performances point, however, again to the prejudiced nature with which natives might study Karl Moik and his show. The latent sexism is precisely one of the elements irritating to parts of the Austrian viewing public. The fact that even migrants who have a perfect knowledge of German and a high level of education feel at least partly excluded from understanding this "insider humour" à la Moik is in itself a noteworthy result of our research project. There are associations that can be used effectively to exclude the meaning of folklore, traditions and regional dialect from anyone who has only been in Austria for a short time; refugees, migrants, new Austrians, or other "threats from below" are effectively excluded in this way (Diaconu 2006: 221–224; cf. also Gingrich 2006b; Gingrich & Banks 2006; Köstlin 2002; Dundes 1985). This is partly explained by the fact that in discussions, both researchers tended to emphasize music as the focal aspect of their investigation of the Musikantenstadl (and less with the presentational style of Karl Moik, that is, *what* he said and *how* he said it). As a result, it is possible that important data on political and identity-forming aspects of the Musikantenstadl were not taken into account.

An interesting and somewhat paradoxical component of the team research experience was the differential value we placed on the selected method: Both foreign researchers were, in general, pleased to investigate the Musikantenstadl in the context of Alpine popular culture. Both, however, were somewhat skeptical about the value of their "outsider's gaze" in the project – even though they had been invited to collaborate mainly because they could bring this "external gaze". Both researchers often pointed out that their view was not so exotic, since they were also shaped by their (western-influenced) higher education and had lived in Austria for several years. Zeynep Baraz pointed out that she had seen such popular television programs as a child in Istanbul and had almost grown up with them. Mădălina Diaconu went as far as to criticize the degree of culturalism in the research design – both in terms of assuming a primordial cultural understanding and in the differentiation between "foreigners" and "locals". As the research progressed, I became aware that it was maybe only really clear and indisputable for us native ethnologists coordinating the project that being a foreigner could be something positive in the research process. "We" saw unfamiliarity as a crucial and essential key to understanding the culture. Numerous discussions followed in different team meetings in which I tried (with only partial success) to convince the two foreign project team members of the usefulness of the "external or outsider's gaze" – sometimes using examples from my field research practice as detailed in the previous section. We succeeded, eventually, to relativize each other's understanding: The "external or outsider's gaze" must not be misperceived as "understanding nothing"; conversely, a background of migration, being both foreign and socialized into aspects of the researched culture, as well as the academic culture, relativized the outsider's perspective of the foreigners.

The Outsider's Gaze in Cultural Analysis

The objections of the foreign researchers with regard to classifying their own outsider role on the one hand and the "devaluation" of the Stadl by the native researchers on the other hand, necessitates a redefinition and differentiated conceptualizations of outsider status.

The types of outsider experience described by Schäffter (1991) form the basis of the following considerations. He assumes that networks of reciprocal dependencies are close-knit; therefore being an outsider can be a conflict-prone situation in the here and now, rather than at a distance. Estrangement is a quality experienced in relationships (and not a characteristic of people or things). This experience intensifies with proximity and closeness. From this perspective, the Musikantenstadl can be seen as a cultural contact zone between country and city dwellers, purportedly "ordinary people" and the "intellectuals" or – using the Sinus Milieus typology[10] – between the *traditionals and quiet peaceful Britains* and, on the other side, the *precarious*, *pleasure seekers*, *post-materialists*, and *experimentalists*.[11] Which perception of reciprocal outsider status should be expected in encounters such as those necessitated by our project – the Austrian and foreign researcher with the Stadl recipients, the foreign researchers with the Austrian researchers, and so forth? To answer this question it is important to clarify the restrictions from which the cultural, social, and individual identities derive their "singularity" and contrast them with the "others".[12] Schäffter (1991: 11–42) identifies four types of outsider understanding. These are discussed in more detail below:

(1) "Outsider position as a sounding board for oneself": This type mainly appears comprehensible as a result of empathy or affinity emerging when one finds oneself in a new environment. The motto is: "I am not strange – look, the stranger is just like you!" Zeynep Baraz' comment that she had already seen programs similar to the Musikantenstadl as a child in Turkey is reminiscent of this type of understanding.

(2) "Outsider position as a counter-image": This type results from the structuring of social reality with the attendant possibility of wielding power and control. In constructing an inner coherence, based on singularity, it is possible to exclude the stranger as "abnormal". Such an understanding of the other contains within it the danger of a primordial culture relativism – a problem expounded by Mădălina Diaconu. It raises the question of degrees of distance that then permit to be defined as "outside".

(3) "Outsider position as completion": The more complex the sensory system, the less probable it is that selective interpretation models of a dual order can be sustained. Self and outsider are continually redefined by the interaction of assimilation and accommodation.[13] With the prerequisite of compatibility with the self, being an outsider has the instrumental function of an external range that helps to develop the new impulses and offers reasons to learn (Schäffter 1991: 22–23). Applied to the research project *Alpine popular culture*, this would mean that the "external gaze" is used for completion – providing a complete picture of the "Musikantenstadl" phenomenon in the process. Such an approach would be problematic because it looks for an "objective reality" which it surmises in the sum of all different perspectives. To reduce the perceptions of the foreign scholars or the perception of an economist to "usable enhancements" (for social anthropological work), would be problematic for both from ethical and epistemological points of view.[14]

(4) "Outsider position as a complement": This type characterizes an organizing structure containing different individual perspectives, in which the "internal and external" are not treated as separate areas, but are understood as moments in a structuring process in which self and the other mutually qualify and define each other (Schäffter 1991: 25). The world is constructed as a "poly-contextural" universe in which different knowledge is linked to local and social constitution processes. This results in the necessity to accept and be sensitive to mutual differences. The "external gaze" in this type does not ask how "abnormal" or threatening the unknown is. Instead it focuses on the constant swing between internal view and external view.

A social science method that uses the "outsider's gaze" as a research tool, must probably conceptualize the situation of being a stranger in this "complementary" way. It is consequently recognizable as the result of a practice of differentiation in mutual interaction, though it is never completely definable. I consider it unavoidable and vital that the "constant reflection of the outsider's experience" was adhered to in writing in a research diary. This is useful for a critical reflection of one's own conduct in the research process and also for the subsequent interpretation of the collected data.

The Role of the Project Coordinator as an Outsider

For potential, future research projects intent on working with the component of "the external gaze", it will be useful to think through a methodologically necessary dilemma I frequently encountered in my role as project coordinator: To what extent and in what capacity should I involve myself with the ethnographic data collection carried out by the two "foreign" scientists? This question arose in part due to time constraints (the coordination involved a great deal of administrative legwork), but mainly due to the methodology and the research theory it built on. While I did not want to withhold ethnological expertise from the two foreign researchers, it also did not seem appropriate to provide concrete research instructions, develop questionnaires and interview guidelines and point the researchers on their path under the motto of sending out one's "research bees"; furthermore, such a stance would have undermined the "external gaze" which, ultimately, also manifests itself in the ways in which participant observation and interviews are conducted. I tried to find a middle ground, providing the researchers with as much space as needed and, at the same time, to be available for advice and, if desired, a more active involvement in the research process.

The position was, however, not always easy. I often felt a certain pressure from other researchers. I was flooded with good and well-intended advice and special tips on the meaning of the Musikantenstadl; often I was met with consternation because I did not follow these hints myself and instead thanked these voluntary advisors with the words: "I will pass on this information to Mādālina Diaconu and Zeynep Baraz!" Reproaches such as: "Why didn't you … ?" can be answered better when one is in the field and has sole responsibility for ethnography and data analysis from start to finish.

Concluding Remarks

In summary, the methodological concept of the "external gaze" is an excellent approach to become familiar with such "contentious" cultural phenomena as the Musikantenstadl from a scholarly perspective. The "external gaze" enables unusual and varied results that are not restricted to monocausal answers, and that accentuate the complexity of the construction of a social reality. Due to the interdisciplinary nature of our research project – without a social anthropologist in the field – the focus of social anthropological questioning was not a primary objective in the research goals; it would be interesting, even desirable, to tackle such cultural phenomena which arguably exist in every national public culture with foreign ethnologists as part of the team. As ethnologist and team coordinator, I would like to conclude with some observations on the results of the *The Musikantenstadl project*. From a cultural and social anthropological view, I would find it interesting to further investigate the aspects of instrumentalizing "homeland folklore" as discussed by Mādālina Diaconu (2006: 223ff): How is the emphasis of a common historical tradition and the production of dialect, costume, and music a means to exclude, in a "gentle, inconspicuous way", newcomers to Austria? Does the safe world of the Musikantenstadl actually suggest a "real" Austrian identity that is separated from Brussels, and also free from asylum seekers, migrants, and "new Austrians"? How does Austrian chauvinism differentiate itself from the "larger neighbor" Germany, which was mentioned by interview partners in one form or another in almost all interviews held by Zeynep Baraz? And: What role do the "threats from above" play – EU integration and possible fears connected with US hegemony – in fostering attachment to a program like the Stadl?

One surprising insight gained from the economic research component of the project concerns the extremely high target group orientation employed by the Musikantenstadl producers in designing the show. Seen from that perspective, the Musikantenstadl does not need to please everyone. The only important thing is how well it is accepted by the targeted population groups. From a series of interviews that Wolfgang Fellner carried out with decision makers at ORF, it became clear that they themselves are also not necessarily great fans of this program. The ORF is funded in part through a public learning contract and there is relatively little leeway in program development. There is a relatively high demand for formats such as the Stadl and everything aired must be in line with the recent market evaluation, otherwise the ORF would inevitably lose market shares. The producers of the Musikantenstadl thus see very limited scope for negotiation, as they are also committed to the principle of maximum coverage. Seen from outside, it almost looks as though the fact that you "must join in" with the Musikantenstadl does not only refer to the applause and swaying to the music by the audience, but also to the fact that the public broadcaster simply *must* provide programs for this type of audience. From this economic perch, we have the open market and neoliberal politics to thank for the product Musikantenstadl. These interviews (Fellner 2006b: 91–109) show that the primary concern is for viewing figures and associated advertising incomes.

I find it refreshing that in the first and second decade of its existence, the Musikantenstadl kept its distance from nationalism (cf. Gingrich 2006a: 29). However, if I look at this in connection with Fellner's explanation of the decision structures in ORF, I cannot quite abandon the suspicion that the Stadl's emphasis of the transnational and the avoidance of direct nationalistic references is more due to an increase in profits and productivity that due to host Karl Moik's view of the world.

The project results show that it is the social and economic uncertainties of modern life that make the Musikantenstadl successful. Particular social value judgments that may be rare in everyday life of the present, are, according to the results of the research project, retained in the Musikantenstadl: loyalty, security and stability, willingness to help, sociability and protection, family ideals and a harmonious private life with a classic role distribution between men and women, links to the homeland, and last but not least, performance of one's duties. The social norms and values discussed here are particularly important in those population groups that are the target groups of the Musikantenstadl. This is documented in studies of media research as well as the qualitative interviews that were carried out as part of the research project. In the so-called *Stadl family* (to quote Karl Moik), the fans find what is important to them and what they consider to be threatened by present-day globalization influences (cf. Barna 2004: 71–80).

However, the motivation to see the Stadl or to participate in live events cannot be exclusively explained as "returning to the safe world". From an ethnological perspective it became clear to me that for many people, the Musikantenstadl represents a way around their problems. To indulge in some "time out of time" occasionally and to enjoy the ritualistic routine of the Musikantenstadl, to take refuge in a safe, parallel world and "switch off" for a while, offers the chance to dull everyday worries and problems. The Musikantenstadl helps to combat stress. When seen in this way, the Musikantenstadl is not just the *result* of western globalization. It can also be interpreted as a (subjective) *strategy* that helps people to overcome the negative effects of globalization.

"The politicians should not argue so much, they should listen to more *Volksmusik* – for music brings people together!" Such apolitical expressions, as often uttered by Karl Moik in "his" Stadl, awake in me associations with the old Marxian notion of religion as "opium of the people". Apolitical is not unpolitical, instead it is perhaps more of a dangerous political substratum. Researching this tangent further is ethnographically challenging. The two "foreign" researchers avoided any comment that would have given any clue as to their personal political disposition. From the institution in charge of the program, I got the impression that a critical confrontation with this cultural phenomenon is undesirable. Working ethnographically with the national media company was a new experience which also holds challenges for research ethics, rather unfamiliar to me compared to my previous field research on popular religion in the Middle East.

What was an additionally new and unfamiliar component for ethnological research in the framework of the Stadl project was the high degree of public interest. We were almost overrun with queries and all project team members made an effort to accommodate journalists asking for interviews. More than thirty newspaper articles appeared in the local press during a period of just three months, and some of these included detailed reports on our project or research results, followed by detailed reports in the most popular weekly and monthly magazines, as well as different radio pieces. This great success in scholarly communication was, without a doubt, also due to the innovative methodological procedures. For ethnology and social anthropology, the "external gaze" offered a unique opportunity to engage the public in dialog.

Notes

1. It was only during the research that the media announced that the contract between ORF and Karl Moik would not be extended from 2006. Moiks "departure" and his last "Stadl" – the New Year's Eve "Stadl" on December 31st 2005 – occured during our project period. In September 2006, a new series of the Musikantenstadl began with the Austrian pop singer Andy Borg as the presenter, and this has brought high viewing figures for ORF.
2. This was a follow-up project to the Wittgenstein research cluster Local Identities and Wider Influences which was established at the Social Anthropology Unit. The present research project was funded by the two Jubilee Funds of the Austrian National Bank (ÖNB) and the municipality of Vienna (MA 7). Prof. Dr. Andre Gingrich, Chairman of the Social Anthropology Unit, was the project leader. The Austrian social anthropologists Mag. Dr. Susanne Binder and Mag. Dr. Gebhard Fartacek were responsible for the coordination of the project contents and organization. Scientific colleagues: DDr. Mădălina Diaconu (born and raised in Romania; main research areas: Art philosophy and anthropology of senses) and MMag. Zeynep Baraz (born and raised in Turkey; main research areas: Media sociology and migration research). The two "foreign" researchers were supported by the Viennese economist Mag. Wolfgang Fellner who provided media-economic data on the Musikantenstadl and enabled close cooperation with ORF.
3. For helpful comments on various aspects of this article, I thank Regina Bendix (Göttingen) and Andre Gingrich (Vienna).
4. The full project results have been published in Susanne Binder and Gebhard Fartacek's book *Der Musikantenstadl: Alpine Populärkultur im fremden Blick* [The Musikantenstadl: An Outsider's Gaze of Alpine Popular Culture] (Münster, LIT Verlag, 2006).
5. For a sociolinguistic perspective on how to, conversely, achieve the capacity to ask in locally appropriate ways in extended fieldwork situations, cf. Briggs (1981).
6. At this point, it should be mentioned that the budget for the research project was very tight due to cutbacks by the Austrian National Bank through whose competitive research division the project was funded. As a result, the foreign project colleagues could only be employed for 12 months (at 15 hours/week) instead of 2 years as originally planned.
7. Germans who were forced to leave their former homelands in Poland, Bohemia and Silesia after World War Two occasionally refer to themselves as "Sudeten-Deutsche" after the mountains located in those regions. These associations have a difficult history and an often problematic political positioning, and the stereotypical ambience of such groups is – in some corners of the public imagination – of a kind with the Stadl.
8. The contributions assembled in the volume Inspecting Germany (Hauschild & Warneken 2002) pursued an agenda quite similar to our project – non native scholars were to provide their insights on German culture, through the at once alienating and revealing mirror of the outsider's gaze.
9. This is all the more surprising as the Belgian film maker Nathalie Borgers had recently done a revealing, highly critical documentary of the main tabloid paper in Austria, entitled *Kronen Zeitung – Tag für Tag ein Boulevardstück* (Kronen Zeitung – Day by Day a Boulevard Play). The film-maker at first had the complaisant support of her "victim" which explains the freely provided information from the individual editors (including Hans Dichand). Borgers' methodological process resembles that of the investigative journalism of the German author Günther Wallraff.
10. Sinus Milieu is a term used in marketing research, derived from the notion of "social milieus" introduced by Émile Durkheim. Our project adopted the term not least because it is a frequently used concept in marketing a new product – here for instance the Stadl – to viewers or buyers.
11. For a methodological critique of this artificial classification, see Fellner (2006a: 61–69; cf. 2006b: 77–118), who following Schülein (2002) highlights the necessity of connotative theories in the context of autopoetic reality.
12. In this context, identity is defined as a component of social "reality" and not as a part of an (unchangeable) human nature. It is the result of the characteristics of social situations, interactional conditions, and available cultural knowledge. One and the same person or group "owns" not just one identity but several identities, for example a cultural, regional, national, ethnic, religious, and gender identity, or identities based on occupation and economic and social situations. A person or group can simultaneously have hegemonic and minority positions. Identity is conceptualized as the result of processes of internal and external attribution with both cognitive and emotional components. Finally, both local and transnational processes are relevant for the production of affiliations and dissociation.
13. In the sense of Piaget, *accommodation* is the modification of a cognitive schema to new experiences. In contrast, *assimilation* is the integration of an object of human experience in a cognitive schema.
14. It is common for types (1), (2) and (3) that confrontation with the foreigner is not conducted in a partnership dialog because foreignness plays an important role in developing and sustaining identity.

References

Agar, Michael 1980: *The Professional Stranger. An Informal Introduction to Ethnography*. New York: Academic Press.

Altheide, David L. 1996: *Qualitative Media Analysis*. Thousand Oaks, London, New Delhi: Sage.

Baraz, Zeynep 2006: Soziologie der Unterhaltung. In: S. Binder & G. Fartacek (eds.), *Der Musikantenstadl: Alpine Populärkultur im fremden Blick*. Wien, Münster: LIT-Verlag, 119–154.

Baraz, Zeynep & Mădălina Diaconu 2006: Die volkstümliche Musik des Musikantenstadls in Beziehung zu nahöstlichem Arabesk und südosteuropäischen Manele. In: S. Binder & G. Fartacek (eds.), *Der Musikantenstadl: Alpine Populärkultur im fremden Blick*. Wien, Münster: LIT-Verlag, 229–248.

Barna, Gabor 2004: Religion as a Shelter. *Ethnologia Europaea*, Vol. 34, No. 1, 71–80.

Baumann, Zygmunt 2002: Der Pilger und seine Nachfolger: Spaziergänger, Vagabunden und Touristen. In: P.-U. Merz-Benz & G. Wagner (eds.), *Der Fremde als sozialer Typus. Klassische soziologische Texte zu einem aktuellen Problem*. Konstanz: UVK Verlagsgesellschaft mbH, 163–187.

Briggs, Charles 1995 (1981). *Learning how to Ask*. Cambridge: Cambridge University Press.

Diaconu, Mădălina 2006: Zur Ästhetik des Musikantenstadls. In: S. Binder & G. Fartacek (eds.), *Der Musikantenstadl: Alpine Populärkultur im fremden Blick*. Wien, Münster: LIT-Verlag, 155–228.

Dundes, Alan 1985: Nationalistic Inferiority Complexes and the Fabrication of Folklore. *Journal of Folklore Research* 22, 5–18.

Fartacek, Gebhard. 2003a: *Pilgerstätten in der syrischen Peripherie. Eine ethnologische Studie zur kognitiven Konstruktion sakraler Plätze und deren Praxisrelevanz*. (Sitzungsberichte der phil.-hist. Klasse 700. Band; Veröffentlichungen zur Sozialanthropologie Nr. 5). Wien: ÖAW-Verlag.

Fartacek, Gebhard 2003b: Der Approach der Fallrekonstruktion und seine methodische Umsetzung am Beispiel ethnographischer Erhebungen in Syrien. In: G. Fartacek & E. Halbmayer (eds.), *Methodenfragen der Kultur- und Sozialanthropologie: Historische und Sozialwissenschaftliche Beiträge*. Working Papers der Kommission für Sozialanthropologie, Reihe A: Lokale Identitäten und überlokale Einflüsse. Wittgenstein 2000, Band 6, Wien: ÖAW-Verlag [Online Edition, DOI 10.1553/witt2k6, http://hw.oeaw.ac.at/wittgenstein_2000?frames=yes] 32–38.

Fartacek, Gebhard 2006: Der "fremde Blick" im Rückblick: Methodologische Betrachtung und Kommentar zu den Untersuchungsergebnissen. In: S. Binder & G. Fartacek (eds.), *Der Musikantenstadl: Alpine Populärkultur im fremden Blick*. Wien, Münster: LIT-Verlag.

Fellner, Wolfgang 2006a: Die volkstümliche Musik in Zahlen – empirische Grundlagen der Medienforschung. In: S. Binder & G. Fartacek (eds.), *Der Musikantenstadl: Alpine Populärkultur im fremden Blick*. Wien, Münster: LIT-Verlag, 32–76.

Fellner, Wolfgang 2006b: Die ökonomischen Hintergründe der Fernseh-Unterhaltung am Beispiel des Musikantenstadls. In: S. Binder & G. Fartacek (eds.), *Der Musikantenstadl: Alpine Populärkultur im fremden Blick*. Wien, Münster: LIT-Verlag, 77–118.

Flick, Uwe 1995: *Qualitative Forschung – Theorien, Methoden, Anwendung in Psychologie und Sozialwissenschaften*. Reinbek bei Hamburg: Rowohlt.

Gingrich, Andre 2004: Conceptualising Identities: Anthropological Alternatives to Essentialising Difference and Moralizing about Othering. In: G. Baumann & A. Gingrich (eds.), *Grammars of Identity/Alterity. A Structural Approach*. London, New York: Berghahn, 3–17.

Gingrich, Andre 2006a: Alpine Populärkultur in globalisierten Zeiten: Methodische Reflexionen und Einsichten. In: S. Binder & G. Fartacek (eds.), *Der Musikantenstadl: Alpine Populärkultur im fremden Blick*. Wien/Münster: LIT-Verlag, 24–31.

Gingrich, Andre 2006b: Urban Crowds Manipulated: Assessing the Austrian Case as an Example in Wider European Tendencies. In: R. Pinxten & E. Preckler (eds.), *Racism in Metropolitan Areas*. London, New York: Berghahn.

Gingrich, Andre & Marcus Banks (eds.) 2006: *Neo-Nationalism in Western Europe and Beyond: Perspectives from Social Anthropology*. London/New York: Berghahn.

Hauschild, Thomas & Bernd Jürgen Warneken (ed.) 2002: *Inspecting Germany. Internationale Deutschland-Ethnographie der Gegenwart*. Münster: Lit-Verlag.

Köstlin, Konrad 2002: Bräuche und Identitätsstiftung. Landesverband Salzburger Volkskultur. Manuskript.

Luger, Kurt 1990: Mozartkugel und Musikantenstadl. Österreichs kulturelle Identität zwischen Tourismus und Kulturindustrie. *Medien Journal. Life Style. Zeitschrift für Kommunikationskultur der ÖGK*, 14. Jg., Heft 2, 79–96.

Oppitz, Michael 1993: *Notwendige Beziehungen. Abriß der strukturalen Anthropologie*. Frankfurt am Main: Suhrkamp.

Schäffter Ortfried 1991: Modi des Fremderlebens. Deutungsmuster im Umgang mit Fremdheit. In: O. Schäffter (ed.), *Das Fremde. Erfahrungsmöglichkeiten zwischen Faszination und Bedrohung*. Opladen: Westdeutscher Verlag, 11–42.

Schülein, Johann August 2002: *Autopoietische Realität und konnotative Theorie: Über Balanceprobleme sozialwissenschaftlichen Erkennens*. Weilerswist: Velbrück Wiss.

Steinke, Ines 2003: Gütekriterien qualitativer Forschung. In: U. Flick, E. Kardorff & I. Steinke (eds.), *Qualitative Forschung*. Reinbeck: Rowohlt, 319–331.

Strauss, Anselm 1991: *Grundlagen qualitativer Sozialforschung – Datenanalyse und Theoriebildung in der empirischen soziologischen Forschung*. München: Fink.

Dr. Gebhard Fartacek is researcher and deputy director of the Social Anthropology Research Unit at the Austrian Academy of Sciences [Österreichischen Akademie der Wissenschaften ÖAW]. His latest publication is *Unheil durch Dämonen? Geschichten und Diskurse über das Wirken der Djinn im Nahen Osten. Eine ethnologische Spurensuche* [Cursed by Demons? Stories and discussions on the function of the Djinn in the Middle East. An ethnological search] (2007, in press). His current research focuses on cosmologies, religious belief systems, and local strategies for conflict resolution in the Middle East, epistemological subject models as well as methods of empirical social research.
(gebhard.fartacek@oeaw.ac.at,
http://www.oeaw.ac.at/sozant)

THE CAMINO DE SANTIAGO
The Interplay of European Heritage and New Traditions

Dani Schrire

> In this paper I discuss different ideals shaping the development of the reanimated Camino de Santiago (the pilgrim routes to Santiago de Compostela). I first analyze the heritage ideal, represented by the official discourse, especially that of the Council of Europe. I then look at the ideals represented by the material route signs, which demonstrate how the European heritage discourse is enacted "from below" together with competing ideals of the Camino. Last, I present modern traditions found on the Camino and the implicit ideals underlying them. I argue that these traditions are transmitted by face-to-face conduct (orally and bodily) as well as through written texts (mainly on the Internet). I conclude with remarks on the nature of these traditions and their interplay with the European heritage ideal.
>
> *Keywords*: Camino de Santiago, tradition, heritage routes, cultural routes, post-nationalism

On my first Camino (Camino de Santiago or the Way of St. James) in 2000 I passed through the small village of Tiebas. I took a look around its municipal pilgrim hostel (*albergue*), hoping someone might stamp my pilgrim passport. It was half way to that day's destination – Puenta La Reina, where the Camino Aragonés joins the crowds on the Camino Francés. The door of the albergue was shut, but a note was placed on it. It was a note thanking the village people for their hospitality, put up by the Muslim Amigos of the Camino de Santiago en route to one of Christianity's main patrons, St. James (the elder), who was also known as the guardian of the Christians in their war against the Spanish Moors. I was wondering how Muslims could walk along a route, where occasionally St. James is depicted in a typical iconography known as *Santiago Matamoros* (St. James the Moor-slayer). This question touches on one of the many contradictions and puzzles posed by the reanimation of the pilgrim routes to Santiago de Compostela.

By the time I set off on my second journey on the Camino in the holy year of 2004,[1] the term "the Camino" represented many thousands of kilometers adorned with unique Camino symbols and signs that can be found across Europe (especially in Spain and France, but as far as Italy, Poland and Holland). In the 1,300 kilometers of Camino mileage I walked, and the thousands I drove, I listened to many stories and I spent hours reading many more in the imagined Camino community on the Net or in books. My own experiences drew my attention to the Camino's diverse character, which raised many questions that I addressed to myself as much as I addressed them to others.

Why do people in the twenty-first century go on pilgrimage by foot to a city in north-west Spain? This wasn't always so. Dunn and Davidson (1996), who have been following the Camino since the 1970s, tried to explain the change it had gone through (p. xlvi):

… in 1974 … When we arrived at the Cathedral, we had some trouble finding the Cathedral archivist for the *Compostela* certificates. His book listing pilgrims for that year had fewer than fifty names … What a difference in 1993! 99,000 pilgrims … In these twenty years I feel that I have witnessed and participated in the rebirth of a phoenix.[2]

In my research I focused on the life of this "phoenix" after its rebirth. In this paper I discuss the ideals shaping the contemporary Camino (explicit and implicit). I do that by examining three discourses on the Camino. First, I discuss the official heritage discourse (represented by the Unesco and the Council of Europe) and its *conceptual* idea of heritage routes. Then I examine the *material* discourse represented by the Camino route signs and symbols, including the (normative) discourse about them. Last, I analyze a few traditions of the reanimated Camino as evident in books, pilgrim forums and voices I heard on my own Caminos, by emphasizing their *verbal* articulation and the *bodily* movement involved in their experience.

Context

Most historians trace the discovery of the Galician tomb of St. James (who was beheaded in Jerusalem in 44 AD) to the ninth century, when a farmer was directed by a falling star to a field that revealed the tomb (hence it is known today as *Compostela* – "field of stars"). Historians discuss the massive popularity of the pilgrimage to the shrine in the Middle Ages, a place which became a very important Christian pilgrim destination in the twelfth century, third only to Rome and Jerusalem (Stokstad 1978). Many of these historians emphasize the role of "the pilgrim's guide", the Codex Calixtinus, a Latin manuscript written in the twelfth century. This manuscript, attributed to Aymeric Picaud, a French monk from Poitiers, describes four pilgrim paths in France: three merge at the foothills of the Pyrenees and another, the Camino Aragonés, crosses the Pyrenees on a higher pass and joins them into a single pilgrim's path, in Puenta La Reina (Navarre). Historians of the Camino tend to recognize specific places and thereby create an historic picture of standard pilgrim routes.

Recently, this historical account was undermined by Denise Péricard-Méa (2000), who denies the importance of the Codex Calixtinus. Although it was written in the twelfth century, she doubts its popularity in the Middle Ages and points out that it was discovered only as late as the nineteenth century. She discusses the multiplicity of the cult of St. James in the Middle Ages, which went far beyond his tomb in Compostela, and traces the "invention" of many of the accepted medieval pilgrim traditions to the literature of the Counter-Reformation and to the scholars of the nineteenth and twentieth centuries. Based on different pilgrim accounts, she demonstrates the varying motivations for the pilgrimage, as well as the different routes taken by pilgrims in the Middle Ages.

Historians do not doubt the popularity of the legends connected to St. James' shrine as these were well known. None however, argue the fact that the pilgrimage died almost completely by the nineteenth century and was reanimated only in the last thirty years. This revival has received considerable academic (and non-academic) attention from various points of departure.

Thus, it is considered by Lois González and Somoza Medina (2003: 450) as "Northern Spain's main tourist product".[3] If the Camino is a "product" then one wonders: who are its producers? I would argue that many pilgrims and people who are connected to the Camino do not view it as a "product" per se and the Camino was not an outcome of the work of a great business firm.

In their discussion of heritage routes, Moulin and Boniface (2001) imply that such routes are more than "business", and that they "… have social aims as well as economic goals" (p. 237). In relation to the Camino, they mention that "One aspect of the pilgrimage from the past … is that the pilgrimage involves shared effort and represents a *common ideal*" (ibid.: 241, my italics).

This "common ideal" is left a bit vague. While there might be a common destination, many pilgrims do not arrive there. If there is a common ideal, then it differs between the Camino's different "producers" (in Lois González and Somoza Medina's terminology) – whether these are heritage officials in Strasbourg or Paris, or whether they are restaurant owners in Astorga or a Brazilian pilgrim debating her love life in El-Acebo. In this paper, I relate to some of the ideals (in the plural form), that are involved in shaping the contemporary Camino, and are revealed through the examination of three discourse types.

Heritage Talks

The concept of "heritage" played a decisive role in the Camino's rebirth. It was utilized by two heritage institutions, the Council of Europe and the Unesco, whose discourse is analyzed here.

In 1987 the Council of Europe designated the Camino as the first European Cultural Route. Until then, the Camino was an esoteric phenomenon, and though a spark was already lit – as 2,000 pilgrims walked to Compostela that year – it was still a drop in the ocean in comparison to the Camino in the 1990s. By 1993 the Unesco had the Spanish route included in its World-Heritage list, and parts of the French routes were added in 1999 along with a list of specific structures.

What does it mean for a route to become heritage? The tangible features of the Camino – churches, Christian Medieval art, Roman pavements, etc., mentioned in Unesco's World-Heritage list – might explain why a series of structures are considered "heritage material". Some of the monuments are in Romanesque style while others are in Baroque or Gothic styles. These monuments presumably together tell an historical story, which is diachronic. It is not clear whether the space between the monuments is considered "heritage material" as well: roads, modern buildings, etc. In other words, Unesco's idea of a (linear) route is not very clear; is it like in a child's game – "connecting the dots"?

In their guidelines to the inscription of specific types of properties on the World-Heritage list, Unesco's definition of a heritage route is stated as follows: "A heritage route is composed of tangible elements of which the cultural significance comes from exchanges and a multi-dimensional dialogue across countries or regions, and that illustrate the interaction of movement, along the route" (Unesco 2005: 88). This definition is further elaborated (ibid.: 89, original italics):

> The concept of heritage routes is based on the dynamics of movement and the idea of the *exchange*, with *continuity* in space and time; refers to a *whole*, where the route has a worth over and above the sum of the elements making it up and through which it gains its cultural significance; highlights exchange and dialogue *between countries or between regions*; is *multi-dimensional* …

Note that the route is based on tangible heritage, but though it is not stated clearly, it is evident that the route is *also* based on intangible features which represent the idea of exchange and international/interregional dialogue that elevates the tangible "elements" to a "whole" route.

When Unesco added the Spanish route it was noted that: "it is a 'living' route, *still* used by countless pilgrims" (my italics), in what gives the impression of an unchanged Camino in History's *longue durée*. The implicit intangible elements are explicitly discussed in Unesco's document for the justification of the State Party in the case of the French routes to Compostela – it mentions the Medieval *chansons de geste* as an example for non-tangible north-south dialogue existing on the Camino. As Peter Robins notes,[4] this designation is quite problematic since it is based on a few strange assumptions such as that the valuable monuments found on the routes are necessarily connected to the Camino.

The Council of Europe departs from Unesco's approach in understanding cultural routes by emphasizing mainly intangible heritage. European scholars had been engaged in documenting the historical Camino for some time – the French Société des Amis de Saint-Jacques was established in 1950 and one of its founders, René de La Coste-Messelière, had already emphasized the European qualities of the routes to Santiago de Compostela (see Péricard-Méa 2000). However, Spain's entrance to the EC in 1986 and the opening of its borders marked (for the Camino) an important shift from nation-centered politics to European politics. European political-cultural institutions began to get an interest in the Camino in the middle of the 1980s. A memorandum published by the Council for Cultural Co-Operation of the Council of Europe published in March 1987, discussed publicly the idea of European cultural routes. This statement was finalized by the Committee of Ministers' resolution 98(4) from 1998. The Camino was chosen to be the first European cultural route and its implementation was coordinated at first by the Council of Europe and then by the European Institute for Cultural Routes (EICR) in Luxembourg. Most of the European institutionalized intervention in the Camino was not financial, but rather it functioned as a facilitator for cooperation between different partners.[5] This bureaucratic procedure eclipses the fact that these European decision makers have a certain ideology as to what a European Cultural Route should normatively consist of. When I interviewed Michel Thomas-Penette, the director of the EICR, in 2002, he expressed his concern about the fact the Camino is not appreciated as a European cultural route as much as it is seen by pilgrims as a Spanish cultural route. At the time, the European route signs (see a later section) were not visible in France and his concern may have been justified.

The EICR (and their partners) constantly reflect on the meaning of "heritage", "European heritage", "common heritage", etc. Some quotations gathered from the EICR official website reveal this reflective heritage discourse: "a whole dimension of the approach to heritage is constituted by sensible experience ...", "Heritage is a medium"; "how does one interpret cultural heritage in European terms? ... by taking into account the multicultural dimension of heritage and the plural dimension of its visiting (if it is a monument) or of its practice (if it is a tradition, know-how, a festival)".[6] It is interesting to examine these quotations in light of Barbara Kirshenblatt-Gimblett's assertion (1995: 369–370), that "heritage ... produces something new in the present that has recourse to the past" – *prima facie* the European discourse is about the present; the EICR promotes a heritage of people and their movement, thus emphasizing values of cultural exchange cutting across many countries in Europe. This is evident in the chosen themes: Vikings and Normans, Celts, Silk-Textile, Monastic Influence, Hanseatic Sites, European Jewish heritage, the Gypsies, Northern Lights, Castellan language and Sephardic people in Mediterranean areas, the Legacy of Al-Andalus etc. Today there are almost thirty chosen themes. The Camino is part of a broader theme – the pilgrim pathways, although it used to be a theme of its own. In the EICR's "campaign diary", Michel Thomas-Penette (2000) explains the meaning of a cultural route as it is referred to by the Council of Europe (p. 111) – "[it] is not only a physical itinerary, even when it is practiced on specific sites, and even if there are quite a few cases when such an itinerary follows ... a cultural route is characterized by a great European topic ...". And indeed the EICR partners are involved mainly in the promotion of what can be described as intangible heritage, contrary to the tangible heritage emphasized by Unesco.[7] Intangible heritage can create what Johler described (2002: 16) as "European places", which must "be provided on site with symbolic meaning and charged by European content by means of ritual".

As Kirshenblatt-Gimblett (2005: 2) points out: the heritage discourse (in our case, of the Camino) can "change the relationship of people to what they do". However, in my experience of the Camino, the language of heritage, which is "value added" (Kirshenblatt-Gimblett 1995), is not always so appreciated by the people who "do" the Camino. In the creation of European culture, which goes beyond the nation or the region and their memories, the concept of heritage stresses the mediation involved with a possibility of harnessing it to a multi-cultural form of Europeanness. The fact that heritage is considered by some people in the EICR as a medium illustrates that it is seen as the means and not as the end. Perhaps the heritage discourse seems to be "selling" a product, while some of the pilgrims do not want to experience the Camino in such a way. The value people attach to the Camino is made more often by the concept of tradition, which generates to some a positive "added value". The Camino signs represent a varied discourse that combines notions of heritage and of tradition.

Talking with Signs, Speaking of Symbols

Route signs create a mosaic of meanings and represent the different motivations and ideals found on the Camino. Different groups in various spatial scales use different route signs – some emphasize a certain heritage, while some are driven by other motivations.

The scallop shell was associated for centuries with St. James and with the Jacobean cult. Although it is not clear whether it was accepted as a symbol of St. James as early as the twelfth century or a few centuries later (see Almazán 1996), there is no doubt about its pre-Christian origin, as was already suggested by Peake (1919). The revival of the Camino made the scallop shell very popular and it is seen in many contexts – on pilgrims' hats and clothes, on church doors, menus, in hotels and as route signs such as the concrete pole found near Oloron Ste-Marie in the Atlantic Pyrenees (France). Many consider it as the "authentic" symbol of the pilgrimage. In some cases regional governments make use of it in their route signs; sometimes private Camino money-makers use it as an identity badge. Occasionally it is promoted by church officials or by civil associations that support the idea of the pilgrimage – such as the British Confraternity of St. James (CSJ), one of many groups that appeared in the last fifty years (Dunn & Davidson 1996: xxxv–xxxvi). The CSJ mention in their website that: "The scallop shell was and still is the emblem of the pilgrimage, carried back by the proud pilgrim as proof of the successful completion of the long and arduous journey to the shrine of St James."

The European symbol (or rather logo) for the Camino was promoted in 1993 and it is a modernized version of the scallop shell, with straight lines, "European colors" (usually, yellow shell on a blue background) and it is found in at least five countries on different routes. In the area of Jaca (Aragon), volunteers of the European Voluntary Service for Young People worked on stretches of the Camino in Aragon and emphasized the European symbols. However this symbol was adopted voluntarily by various groups who are not identified as "European" in the narrow sense ("European bodies") and yet identify with the

Ill. 1: "Classic" shell in France. (Photo by the author.)

European shell: in Chartres, near Paris, a scallop shell with a sign directing visitors to Compostela is placed in front of its renowned cathedral, hinting at the existence of something (perhaps) more wonderful 1,625 kilometers away. Chartres' municipality is perhaps telling the tourists who come to visit their heritage, the famous glass-windowed cathedral, that this is only a fraction of a bigger – more important – (European) heritage.

The next popular route sign, found especially in Spain and in some other places as well, is a yellow arrow. This index stresses the idea that today's Camino is a one-way network of routes (though if millions of pilgrims did flock to Compostela during the Middle Ages, then they must have had to walk back, something the choice of an arrow obscures). The arrow was introduced by a priest who lived (and was buried) in Galicia and who was one of the main protagonists in the pilgrimage revival, the late Fr. Elías Valiña Sampedro. His deeds remind us of the church's vital role in promoting the Camino as part of what

Frey describes (1998: 246–247) as a shift from a "theology of fear" to a "theology of love": "the Camino as a positive return to the sacred and an ideal means of cultivating faith among European youth" (ibid.).

Another common route sign found in France and Spain is the red-white striped sign promoted by walkers' organizations such as the Fédération française de la Randonnée Pédestre (FFRP). It represents a GR route (a long-distance path) that is not unique to the Camino. Unlike the arrow, its symmetrical structure stresses the idea that the Camino, like any other walking path, can be walked in both directions. I came across some arrow-styled signs of the *Jakobsweg* in Switzerland, though these signs pointed in both directions, so they are similar in their nature to the red-white stripes.

One has to remember that there are different ways to signpost the Camino and that practices such as naming of streets, hotels and apartment projects contribute to the efforts of transforming a series of locales to a web of routes.

In its booklet of practical suggestions (Mayol 2004), the Association Compostelle Inter-Regional mentions these different signs. However, it attaches to them a different value: according to them the signs promoted by the FFRP are less genuine than the European shell. This is consistent with what I heard from other people such as a French couple I met in Le-Puy who attached stickers of the European shell all the way from Lyon to Le-Puy. When I asked them about the FFRP marking, they completely dismissed them as non-Camino signs, but signs for walkers who are no different than other GRs such as the one traversing Corsica. They had no doubts regarding the European stylized symbol they were promoting as members of the *Amis de Saint-Jacques* (the well established French civil association comprised of many regional groups). In fact, they proudly men-

Ill. 2: European shell in Auch (France) – closed side pointing the direction. (Photo by the author.)

tioned the European quality of this symbol and of the Camino being a European Cultural Route.

It is interesting to notice that the very common European shell (specifically) was adopted by different people with different motivations. For example, it appears on a Spanish coin of 100 pesetas from 1993 (kept in my wallet), where on one side the European shell is impressed next to an inscription: "Camino de Europa". On the other side one can observe a basic pilgrimage map with the inscription: "Camino de Santiago". Moreover, though it was promoted on an international scale, it carries a different indexical meaning (on indexicality in signs see Scollon & Wong-Scollon 2003). In most cases, the French, German and Swiss put the shell with its closed side facing the walking direction, whereas the Spanish put it the other way round. A French Camino activist mentioned that it is very important since the European shell signifies the many paths that lead to one point and that for some reason the Spanish do not realize it. The Spanish see it as an icon of the Saint's hand pointing in the right direction.

These signs represent the diverse discourse on the Camino and the way its heritage is seen differently by people who share its revival as an ideal. In the Basque village of Ostabat (the road-sign to the village is adorned with the European shell), where three important Camino paths meet according to the "pilgrim's guide" found in the Codex Calixtinus, a monument and a sign commemorate this "meeting point". However, in the Codex Calixtinus, the Basques are depicted as Barbarians, speaking the language of the devil. By signposting the meeting of the roads, it seems that the local Basques affirm the authority of the Codex, but the sign is placed next to a *Pilota* court (Basque ball game; an important representation of Basque nationalism)[9] and greets pilgrims in English, French, Spanish and Basque.

Ill. 3: European shell in Navarre (Spain) – open side pointing the direction and a yellow arrow. (Photo by the author.)

After giving some background to the importance of the place, the sign reads:

> In the 12c, the "Pilgrim's Guide" by Aymeric Picoud described the Basques as "Barbarians" ... this gives a good indication both of the isolation felt by the exhausted pilgrim, confronted by an unknown language and the mistrust of the Basque people ... the Basque language known as Euskara is one of the oldest languages in Europe ...

In what follows, there is a small introduction to basic Basque words. This sign first acknowledges the heritage of the Camino by stressing its official history as portrayed in the Codex, but then re-contextualizes it so as to fulfill its role in the Basques' (national) heritage.

The sign in Ostabat demonstrates contested identities in the background of the Camino's revival, which normally do not appear on the surface. However, the *choices between* different route signs (as the cases of the European shell and the GR-walking signs demonstrate) represent the struggles over the identity of the Camino as the following example shows very vividly: In 2006, the Galician government announced that they would replace the yellow arrows with a new route sign promoting the holy year of 2010, a big foot symbol, something that follows their work in the holy year of 1999 when they promoted a cartoonish symbol of the Camino. The new decision was a very "hot" topic in some of the pilgrim forums such as the *Santiagobis* forum:[10] "… it makes a mockery of the pilgrimage" wrote one pilgrim and another suggested that "the yellow arrows will win"; another gave an interpretation: "the footprints are … not very functional" whereas the yellow arrow is "the lowest common denominator. All function, no flash". A pilgrim that was not so convinced added: "Somehow I get the feeling … that a lot of people are overreacting … The arrows are not exactly an ancient tradition. They have been around for only thirty years … I have strong feelings for the arrows myself."

The signposting of the Camino is not only about helping tired pilgrims find their way. The different signs represent various ideals and competing Camino identities: European, religious, regional, etc. The discourse *about* this choice demonstrates the emotions involved and the varied justifications for it.

Tradition Conversations: Performance, Text and Words

I am interested in discussing traditions that can be found in the "revived" Camino. My point of departure is similar to that of Simon Colman and John Elsner (2004), who examined the tradition of journeying to Walsingham (Norfolk), and maintain (p. 275) "that a top-down approach to invented tradition is not sufficient to explain much of the contemporary use of tradition by pilgrims at Walsingham". They address here, Eric Hobsbawm's (1983) well known terminology of "invention" that relates primarily to national traditions.[11]

I am aware that naming a few social practices as traditions by a folklorist is in itself a scholarly practice that does not hold a neutral stance towards its object of inquiry. What happens when the term "traditional" is applied as part of a post-modernist discourse? If tradition is modernity's otherness as Pertti Anttonen emphasized in his seminal book (2005), then I believe it holds a more complicated reference to post-modernity. If, as Anttonen argues, tradition is bound to modernity and the nation-state, then what happens to this concept in a post-modernist discourse? This terminology is not aimed at expressing a change in the actual practice, but a change in the researcher's gaze. Anttonen points out that tradition and modernity are not dichotomous notions (ibid.: 39), and so I do not want to transform one novelty into a tradition by emphasizing a new novelty. Rather, I examine the discourse of pilgrims that makes use of an anti-modern approach when it comes to some of the behaviors found on the Camino.

These Camino traditions are orally and bodily transmitted by pilgrims who meet face-to-face during their actual pilgrimage and they are presented here based on my own experiences on the Camino. However, in the discussion of Coleman and Elsner (1995), it is evident that the experience of pilgrimage is also negotiated by pilgrims before they set off on a pilgrimage and on their return home from it. The physical experience of movement through space is later spread by the pilgrims, in many cases with the help of texts. Thus, Coleman and Elsner maintain in relation to pilgrimage (2002: 8) that: "Text and experience interwine." This point reminds us of the important role of texts in pilgrims' practices and their relation to them. It is important to notice that traditions found on the contemporary Camino are also transmitted in written form – through the Web and through books, including scholarly books. An example of the latter is the book written by Nancy Frey (1998), an anthropologist, who describes the Camino's modern life. Her research examines life on the Camino and the way value is attached to certain aspects of it. She goes in the steps of Eade and Sallnow's (1991) post-Turnerian account of pilgrimage, by showing the diverse (at times competing) discourses on the Camino. Her research was conducted in the 1990s, when the Camino was very much a Spanish single route and the Net was hardly a significant arena for pilgrims to share their views. Frey's book reflects on certain aspects of the Camino, but it also functions as a consolidator of some of the practices there. Due to the authority attributed by readers to scholarly material, such books can function as a point of reference not only to *what happens on the Camino* (descriptive knowledge), but also to *how life should be practiced on the Camino* (normative knowledge): many pilgrims who decide to journey the Camino read material before they set foot on one of its paths – artistic books, history books, travel-guides (on paper or on screen), travel accounts found on the Web or in some cases in paper (e.g. Shirley MacLean's spiritual search led her to walk the Camino and her account of this walk was a bestseller). This knowledge – practical, spiritual, historical or anthropological – contributes to the pilgrims' expectation of the Camino and to their experience there. Thus, a reader who reviewed Frey's book in one of the commercial on-line book shops commented: "I found this book to be very helpful to me as I am in the planning stages of walking El Camino in 2000." Another reviewer proclaims that:

"Anthropologist Nancy Frey has managed to bring the experience to vivid life conjuring the sights, sounds, emotions, exhilarations and disappointments of modern pilgrims as they trek across Spain …"

If my own experiences form my first point of departure, then the discourse that Frey analyzed has evolved and has been transformed by now to form my second point of reference. In other words, the voices Frey documented a decade ago formed a set of practices that are repeated – their modernity and novelty can be replaced now by the concept of tradition.

Another source I refer to is the Net and the presentation of the Camino there. The Camino is negotiated in pilgrim forums and comes to life in the many accounts of the pilgrimage, which spread the personal experiences in words and pictures (even with sound-bytes). The virtual experience of pilgrimage was discussed by MacWilliams (2002) and specifically in the case of the Camino by Biella (2003). However, though there is much to be done in this field, I limited myself here mainly to the virtual manifestation of the Camino in one pilgrim forum, *Santiagobis*, which forms my third main point of reference in the traditions I discuss.

The following traditions are presented as contradictory notions. They are common idealizations as much as they refer to 'real' practices. They refer to an experience of a community of pilgrims as much as they refer to my own Camino experience. I develop these points in the discussion which follows.

Tradition 1: On the Camino, Pilgrims Eat Dinner Together

When in Santa Celia (Aragon), my wife spoke to Bernt, a fellow pilgrim from Germany. I suggested that I'd prepare dinner for the three of us. While I began cooking, a German pilgrim couple made themselves dinner and began eating. When (our) dinner was ready, we sat with a bottle of wine and invited the other German couple (Romy and Michael) to join us. When they heard it was my second Camino, Romy was quite shy and begged our pardon for not knowing the Camino custom of eating together in the evening (it was their first Camino night, she apologized). On the following nights they became strong promoters of this newly learnt "custom". Frey mentions that "through sharing a communal dinner and the day's stories, curing blisters ... there is generally a high level of congeniality among pilgrims ..." (ibid.: 96).

Frey opens her book with a lunch she had with other pilgrims in Santiago de Compostela, having completed her pilgrimage in what she describes as a "memorable lunch" (ibid.: 4). In the *Santiagobis* Internet-forum, pilgrims frequently discuss the Camino tradition of eating meals together – one thread was titled: "memorable meals", which referred to "... more than just the food ...". Mark, a pilgrim, discusses a great experience in a French albergue:

> Almost everyone was French, I didn't speak a word of French, but when I sat down for dinner ... the French guys around had my plate loaded before my fanny hit the bench. My glass was never empty, they tried very hard to include me in conversation and after dinner invited me for Cognac and Cigars.

Seen in the host's eyes, Mary, who served as a *hospitalera* (a volunteer in an albergue) discussed the work and mentioned: "I had my hands full making breakfast, cleaning and then organizing dinner for 18–40 people every night. And I loved every minute!"

Tradition 2: Pilgrims on the Camino Live like a Big (Ideal) Family

While walking with my pack through the hot Meseta, not very far from Sahagun, one of my rucksack's shoulder straps snapped. I was a bit puzzled when suddenly a French pilgrim came to the rescue. He was actually so eager, he wouldn't let me resist while he tried (and succeeded, one should add) to fix my pack. When I thanked him for his good Samaritan deed, he smiled back and dismissed my thanks, saying something about the obviousness of it – something you would expect from a fellow pilgrim. This is demonstrated also in Frey's book in a picture of a pilgrim helping treat the leg of another (ibid.: 98, figure 23). Pilgrims often discuss the solidarity and comradeship found on the Camino, though it did not exist at all times; in some cases groups of pilgrims would be very loud, when others tried sleeping.

James, a pilgrim, tells the following story in the *Santiagobis* forum:

> I was walking the Camino in April/May this year, and at dinner one night, we had to separate two Spanish pilgrims, one a military man and the other a Communist, who were arguing about General Franco, and wanted to fight each other. We laughed over the next few days when we saw them both walking happily together, deep in conversation (but probably not about Franco). They had obviously found their similarities and forgotten their differences.

Like stories of the Spanish Civil War of families who were split between the two sides, this story conveys the message that the gap between nationalism/fascism and communism is not important enough to jeopardize the pilgrim family.

Tradition 3: On the Camino Pilgrims Walk Slowly so that They can Take Time to Think

In the first Camino I was running out of time (my planning wasn't very successful) yet I wanted to complete the journey. My motivation was such that occasionally I'd walk 50 kilometers a day. Cyclists would use the fantastic Camino facilities to zoom through the Camino in a *Tour de France* pace. At times pilgrims (upon hearing I had walked in one day what they did in two days) would be angry at me saying that by racing through the Camino "I lose the whole point of reflection". The idea of making use of the Camino to reflect on life outside the Camino and then being engaged in deep conversations with fellow pilgrims is stressed throughout Frey's work. Frey exemplifies the conflict between "arriving" and living the moment by the story of a pilgrim who (based on an experience) "felt more committed to honor the moment" (1998: 74). She then asserts that: "Moving more slowly and getting into the rhythm of the 'human speed' in which 'each step is a thought' can also affect one's sense of place and experience of the natural landscapes" (ibid.). Gower (2002) demonstrates the "transformative" effect of the Camino, which has two facets – walking and thinking, and later discussing thoughts with pilgrims (or telling stories on returning home). Though it cannot be denied that while walking one has time to think, the thesis concerning the "desired" reflection rhythm is not convincing; it is sometimes harder to reflect when walking slowly with a companion than walking alone quickly. Moreover, people can reflect in libraries, in cafés or while taking a ride on a train. In stressing an "expected" slow walking rhythm, pilgrims follow the Romantic ideal of walking as evident in the work of Edensor (2000) or in Daoism and Zen-Buddhism as evident in the work of Macauley (2001).

Tradition 4: On the Camino Pilgrims Give as Much as They Can

While it is true that the Camino was based on a *donativo* given in the pilgrim albergues, nowadays most of the pilgrim albergues demand a certain amount of money per night. Moreover, most of the albergues in France (in fact these are the same as any walkers' refuge) and the private ones in Spain are profit based. The *menu del Peregrino* is no different than any typical *menu del dia* found in villages out of the Camino in Spain. However, it is very typical to hear sayings such as "exploiting the albergue system" or alternatively "commercializing the Camino". Such statements reveal what is taken as obvious – that the Camino is not about money or commercialization, yet one can argue there are many economic gains from the Camino (and others – religious for example). Moreover, many pilgrims in bygone days were exploited, which assured that pilgrimage destination and stopovers thrived. One pilgrim in *Santiagobis* wrote that: "It's an awful pity that profit and commercialism seem to destroy such a good thing as the Camino." Another upon arriving in Compostela wrote:

> I doubt that I will do the French route again in the future. The route appears to be a victim of its own success. Too many people, and too much commercialism. Albergues painting over the arrows to direct you towards their place and away from others. It would seem that Santiago may be nominated as the patron Saint of Taxi drivers. From Leon on were signs all over offering a taxi lift for your pack to the next city.

Frey mentions in her book, that in some remote Galician areas the locals don't have hot water to shower while the government-built albergues have hot water for the pilgrims. Lois González and Somoza Medina (2003) show how the Camino was used for rural development. One *Gîte* (B&B) owner in France (whose *Gîte* belongs to a French association of Camino oriented *Gîtes* – Halts vers Compostelle) told me, that there are disputes between villages on where the authentic Camino path went through. This results in an increasing diversification of the Camino so that more villages would benefit from the Camino's economic success, and indeed for many locals the Camino is all about making a reasonable living.

Tradition 5: On the Camino Pilgrims Live Closely to Nature

Though some of the monuments along the way are very well known and to some they play a very important dimension of the walk, many pilgrims emphasize living close to nature. Frey claims that: "Estrangement may also be induced when one comes in contact with signs of urban life, which contrast sharply with the experience or union in nature" (1998: 81). Dudley Glover wrote in his Web-diary (September 21, 2004):[12]

> Since I was a biology teacher in my youth, I'm interested in all aspects of Mother Nature. After the sun came out, I saw several *mariposas* (butterflies) flitting among the various wild flowers on the margin of the road ... When I got to the sanctuary, I found a terrific view but no restaurant. It was closed.

Glover's testimony points to the importance of experiencing nature in his detailed description, but he also demonstrates the human existence in it – the

Ill. 4: Pilgrims on the Camino – getting close to nature? (Photo by the author.)

road and the closed restaurant. On the Camino, landscape always includes human intervention, though at times the discourse on it blurs this fact. Since many of the pilgrims on the Camino may not be interested generally in outdoor walking, there is a tendency to overemphasize the naturalness of the Camino. However, this is not followed with the full political implications. As one question in *Santiagobis* demonstrates: "What efforts then can we peregrinos (whom, I think get very close to nature on the Camino) make to persuade governments to participate in global agreements to protect the environment?" This question remained unanswered in the forum – something that testifies to the marginality of the political implications, but remains faithful to the belief that pilgrims get close to nature.

Tradition 6: On the Camino Pilgrims Live a Simple and Modest Life

The Camino people are strong promoters of "the simple life". Instead of "simply" driving their car to work, coming back home, watching television and going to bed, the Camino people "simply" walk, eat and sleep. There is nothing simple about walking 700 km (or more), especially when pilgrims recommend to each other in pilgrim forums what gear to buy, what shoes, sleeping bags, packs – all these very sophisticated pilgrim gear, which help make the Camino doable (some discuss the usage of GPS navigating systems and electric sockets for cell-phones).

Many actions, however, are done in the name of simplicity. Some pilgrims reflect on the "simple life we had on the Camino". Pieter, a Dutch pilgrim in the *Santiagobis* forum, mentions that: "Some members mentioned quite rightfully that: 'The one thing about the Camino is that it teaches you how little you need to survive.'" (Note the way knowledge becomes anonymous, though with electronic search tools of Internet forums it is simple to retrieve the actual members who mention this idea). Pieter adds that:

> The silly thing is that the Camino is not fun: it's hardship, rain, sprained ankles, blisters, no food or ATM machines, snoring and indecent people, sleeping on the ground, horrible toilets, but … it is fun and that's the contradiction as we come to the more pure things of our nature: shelter, food and good company.

He then concludes that: "Pilgrims coming home have difficulty to adopt [i.e. adapt; DS] To integrate the simple life into a complicated life", to which Judith, an American pilgrim gave an anti-consumerist interpretation:

> It would be difficult to live that way all the time … But it is a wake-up call for some of us, that we don't need to collect the "things" that we have been conditioned to buy. Especially in North America where at many celebrations, especially at Christmas, the manufacturers come out with gifts of something new and shiney that we really can't live without!

Though true to many pilgrims, one shouldn't forget that sleeping in bunks is not very different than tourists sleeping in such facilities in walking holidays in the Alps or the Pyrenees. On the other hand, many pilgrims lavish on expensive restaurants and wine and some pilgrims enjoy nights in expensive hotels when possible. As one pilgrim (a judge from Tübingen) told me while we dined on a great dinner – being a pilgrim for him meant staying in hotels (preferably in good ones), eating good food and wine in the evening and enjoying the marvelous local beers during the day. However, very often pilgrims regard such behavior as improper or as undermining the true essence of what a true pilgrim is. Frey writes about the pilgrims who arrive at the end and

Ill. 5: Pilgrims having a rest – part of the consumer society? (Photo by the author.)

transform to tourists – buying clothes and souvenirs. I think this dichotomy is a bit misleading since the same pilgrims are part of the "consumer society" before they arrive at Compostela – by buying walking gear prior to the walk; moreover, one of the main reasons for the "cheap" clothing pilgrims wear and why they refrain from buying such souvenirs is the effort to minimize the weight carried by them. Many pilgrims describe their transformation from being tourists looking for a cheap walking holiday to pilgrims. However, in relation to these stories, Pieter (*Santiagobis*) told a "reverse story":

> A Dutch went a few years ago to St J[ean Pied de Port] walking from Holland. He found it very impressive – as the Pyrenees are – then coming nearer to Santiago (he was followed by a TV-crew) he stopped as he found it too much of a show and too commercial. I think he went back doing the GR 10 along the Pyrenees to the Mediterranean to find some solitude!

This story demonstrates what is obscured in the normative pilgrim discourse. Since many of the walkers to Compostela are not experienced walkers, they do not see the family resemblance of the Camino and other long walks (GRs); hence the GR route signs as discussed above are seen as "something else".

New Traditions: Words and Feelings

It could be argued that the usage of a traditional discourse on the Camino is part of a late Capitalist phase, where tradition is used to sell a product or that it is part of a post-materialist trend (both are presented in Anttonen's work as conceptualizations of the post-modern). My attempt, however, in examining these traditions was not aimed at refuting such judgments, but to make sense of them in a post-nationalist context due to their interplay with the post-nationalist European heritage discourse I discussed in an earlier section.

By focusing on these traditions, which, as quoted above, are perhaps only thirty years old, one has to take into account that some of them are based on older roots – national, Medieval, regional, Christian, etc., or that they are part of a New Age discourse that is quite popular among many pilgrims. Most of all, these traditions are undoubtedly connected to me as a subject who was (is?) a promoter of them. They are partial in their nature – in the sense that not all the people on the Camino follow them and also in so far as they represent only one set of traditions found on the Camino that exists there alongside many other bundles of traditions. Many pilgrims are organized in (religious) groups (in many cases they travel by bus) and hence they share a very different experience. My position towards the Christian tradition of the Camino is one of a non-European Jew, a fact that perhaps explains my fascination with the note left by the Muslim friends of the Camino, which I mentioned at the beginning of this paper. Since most of the pilgrims are European and Christian (not necessarily in a Pascalian manner, which gives priority to religious practice), then they might share a different point of departure than my own. Groups of pilgrims live a more "controlled" Camino where their practices might be regulated by the group organizers or according to traditions that are practiced in these groups outside the Camino. However, the traditions I present here were practiced mostly by "individual" pilgrims who nevertheless may have regarded themselves as part of a "Camino community".

Can one discuss a "Camino people"? Many pilgrims discuss the Camino community. Frey goes in the footsteps of Anderson (1991) to consider it as an imagined community consisting of people whom one never met, but who walked the Camino some time ago. This assertion is supported by Biella's work on the Camino's virtual community (2003) and to some extent by Gower's dissertation (2002) on the story-telling practices of Camino veterans in Camino community gatherings done in the States, which she sees as an extension of the Turnerian *communitas* (an ideal she remains faithful to). None of these writers try to define what kind of community the Camino community is, though Frey notes that "while pilgrims feel themselves as a larger community, they also retain a sense of national identity" (1998: 90). I believe one can relate to a Camino community and I agree with Frey that it has an imagined dimension, which becomes very concrete in the "pilgrim gatherings". This community has its own communicating method – the Net as evident in Biella's work (in the same way the newspaper according to Anderson was highly important in the national community's imagination). In certain ways the Camino community is similar to a fan group (Hills 2002), which is active in creating what it is dedicated to – the Camino. This activity is carried out mostly by people who live outside the Camino, contrary to the "fairy tale activists" in the *Märchenstrasse* – the car-oriented tourist route analyzed by Regina Bendix and Dorothee Hemme (2004) – who live along the route. Hills discusses "cult geographies", which go beyond the text; and in some respects the Camino is a "cult geography" – without *a* text. However, I haven't met anybody who considers herself a "Camino fan" (perhaps because fandom seems so be borrowed from the popular culture jargon, which seems to undermine the basic essence of pilgrimage as pilgrims see it).

I referred here to a "Camino community" as a self-contradictory object, though when one discusses an imagined community it is perhaps self-contradictory in any case. This community is separated by many traits. Frey mentions (in addition to the national affiliation) the mode of travel (walkers versus cyclists), and I would add the route chosen (walkers on the most popular route, the Camino Francés, versus walkers on other routes such as the Camino Aragonés, the Vézelay route etc.), and mostly the language barrier separating pilgrims according to a very basic division on the Camino itself and on the Net: one such example can be found in an address delivered by the CSJ's former Chairman, Laurie Dennett, in a gathering of pilgrims in Toronto on 14 May 2005: [13]

> We feel a particular bond with you on this side of the Atlantic – with both the American Pilgrims on the Camino, formerly the Friends of the Road of Saint James, and with the Little Company of Pilgrims here in Canada [The American and Canadian Camino associations respectively; DS]. Part of this probably results from our shared English language in the Jacobean context of so much Spanish!

I was interested in bringing these Camino traditions while deconstructing them so as to show the way they are adopted in the pilgrims' discourse – written or not – and the way they are rejected at the same time because of their power on the self-image of the Camino folk.

From this list it is apparent that the Camino folk tradition is tightly bound to some of the constitutive images of romantic-nationalism's portrayal of the national spirit: living a slow-going simple life, strong family spirit, modest, non-materialistic, reflexive and rural. It is interesting to note that the pilgrims walk through agricultural land. They do not work the land, but they walk the land, which is a performative act that ties them to the Camino. Wylie (2005) commented on walking as a state of "being with landscape".

These traditions of "simple authentic life" did not characterize the primitive societies that constituted the "other", nor did they refer to people or ancestors in ancient "historical" times. Rather, people today perform their life on the Camino – by living what is considered a "simple and authentic" life. However, this ideal does not live (for most) outside the Camino, at home, and hence many pilgrims return to the Camino to be able to discover the joy of "simplicity" again. Compare that to attempts to find this kind of life elsewhere: Western Ireland in the Irish case (Ó Giolláin 2000) or in a different historical "more authentic" time (Bendix 1997). Walking the Camino challenges modernity by focusing on discontinuity through traditionalization (a break from the expected path from modernity to a "super-modernity", e.g. instead of replacing the car with a spacecraft, replacing the car with the human body) and by focusing on continuity – literally "reciting" the footsteps of others – whether ancient ancestors or people who signposted the Camino a year before.

The spoken language obviously divides pilgrims and separates them from one another contrary to the romantic-nationalist ideal. However, the spoken language makes way to a body language – mainly that of walking, which brings people together. Alternately, as Slavin demonstrates (2003), when there were language problems, it was easier to make sense in some of the conversations by "sticking to concrete and shared experiences" (p. 12). The traditions mentioned above are not only necessarily transmitted orally – they are performed in different actions. So while there may be a difference in table manners, the ideal of sitting together in the evening transcends them and is learned regardless of the language spoken. The traditions come into being thus also by a performative imitation.

The limitations of (re)presentation (and an academic paper is a written representation) reduces the experience to what can be "told" (here in English). It avoids the nod I got from the French pilgrim in the *Meseta*, the wink of the *hospitalero* in St. Jean pied de Port accompanied by his firm and slow movement as he pushed me aside and collected the broken glass from the floor, the smile I received from the nun in Carrion de los Condes while she showed me to my bed with a certain bodily gesture, the movement of pilgrims on the stone floor in the albergue in Castrojeriz, the finger on the nose of the Brazilian pilgrim expecting us all to be quiet as his wife was not feeling well or the Basque pilgrim's face as he served us tasty Spaghetti Carbonara in Los Arcos, the rattle of the plates and the smell of food spread all over the dining room. And yet again, I'm left only with words to describe multi-sensory experience …

Conclusion

The European heritage discourse of the Camino emphasizes a search for a common ideal. Contrary to initiatives that emphasize especially the tangible heritage of the Camino (Unesco), the European initiative is concerned with a dynamic approach to heritage with a constant dialogue between the present performance on the Camino and its past. This ideal is negotiated by Camino activists who use a sign language to mark the Camino routes. The route signposting discourse reveals a diverse understanding of the ideal the Camino represents and the discourse on these signs shows that the introduction of the European route sign is highly regarded by many of the pilgrims. Moreover, it demonstrates the way a heritage discourse that was launched "from above" is enacted "from below" and the way the Europeanness of the Camino is slowly accepted in representing the Camino, though together with competing representations – Christian, Spanish and Galician especially.

The examination of traditions seems to demonstrate another search for a common ideal, by pilgrims. This ideal is shared by many members of the growing Camino community and I described it here in romantic terms. It demonstrates a dialogue between the present and the past, but not in heritage terms. It was not presented here as an opposite of the heritage discourse, but rather it complements it in certain aspects. The Camino traditions presented here are transmitted by the usage of oral communication, written form (especially in the Net), but also with a body language, which overcomes language gaps. I call it "romantic post-nationalism" since its diverse discourse of romanticism does not reinforce a specific national romantic past, though it does not go explicitly against any nationalist or regionalist forms of identity.

After the Madrid terrorist attack, there were calls to replace the statue of *Santiago Matamoros* (St. James the Moor-slayer) with a less offensive depiction of Santiago as a pilgrim. Church officials announced that it would be replaced, but after a public outcry they backtracked and decided to keep it in place. If the romantic ideal of the Camino traditions is close to that of the European common heritage ideal, then it is interesting to follow the course of this romantic-European direction in the future. Where is it leading? Will the Muslim Amigos of the Camino be able to take part in the Camino traditions to come? The European heritage discourse is about multiculturalism, promoting the legacy of Al-Andalus as much as the Spanish Jewish (Sephardic) legacy. These legacies touch on the blind spots, the Camino traditions' shadow – the violent past of the *reconquista* that ended in the forced expulsion of the Muslims and Jews from Spain. The Camino heritage is about a constant dialogue and choices – between different roots and routes – a choice that possibly makes all the difference.[14]

Notes

1. A holy year of the pilgrimage (Xacobeo) occurs when the Saint's holy day – July 25th is a Sunday and it happens in intervals of 11, 6, 5, 6 years. The holy year of 1993 marked the success of the Camino revival and demonstrated the potential of it. The success of the next holy year – 1999 – was not a surprise, but it had given a strong momentum to the phenomena, which by Xacobeo 2004 became a wider phenomenon as many of the pilgrims walked the less traveled routes in Spain, France, Portugal etc.
2. The *Compostela* is a proof of the pilgrimage granted by the Archdiocese of Santiago. Though it has a religious significance, today it is granted to anyone walking at least the last hundred kilometers or cycling the last two hundred and for genuine reasons (i.e. spiritual or religious motives) and for many it is the ultimate souvenir. In 2004 close to 180,000 pilgrims were given the official Compostela, though the actual numbers are a lot higher since many pilgrims did not arrive at the end or did not bother to queue for the church certificate.
3. This approach is shared also by Murray and Graham (1997).
4. Robins: "Camino de Santiago – World Heritage? Cultural Route?" http://www.peterrobins.co.uk/camino/heritage.html. Accessed 22.12.2006.
5. In addition to that, volunteers of the European Voluntary Service for Young People worked on stretches of the Camino in Aragon, and according to Frey (1998), the Council organized a conference in 1988 and funded a committee of experts to advise it. Murray and Graham (1997) mention the influx of funds from European regional development programs such as LEADER.
6. European Institute of Cultural Routes website: http://www.culture-routes.lu/. Accessed 15.12.2006.
7. Though in Unesco's 32nd session, intangible heritage was added to the convention: see Unesco's director general's preface to Unesco's *Museum International* volume dedicated to this decision (Matsura 2004).
8. "Santiago de Compostela: the goal of the pilgrimage", *The Confraternity of Saint James website*, http://www.csj.org.uk/santiago-de-compostela.htm. Accessed 11.12.2006.
9. As evident in the documentary movie by Basque film-director, Julio Medem, *La Pelota Vasca: la piel contra la piedra* (2003; English: *The Basque Ball: Skin Against Stone*; Basque: *Euskal pilota: larrua harriaren kontra*).
10. There are many pilgrim forums – Biella discusses them in his work (2003). These are differed according to language and other affiliations. I found the Santiagobis forum to consist of quite an international crowd as it is not affiliated to a specific national group of Camino activists, though it is "biased" by English speakers, its managers are Dutch and at times other languages are used. See http://groups.yahoo.com/group/Santiagobis.
11. Anttonen stresses it was used in the case of nationalism "to legitimate the consolidation of territorial and administrative control" (2005: 11).
12. Glover: "Road to Santiago", http://www.roadtosantiago.org. Accessed 27.12.2006.
13. "2,000 Years of the Camino de Santiago: Where did It Come From? Where is It Going?", *The Confraternity of Saint James website*, http://www.csj.org.uk/2000-years.htm. Accessed 11.12.2006.
14. I would like to thank Ronnie Ellenblum and Galit Hasan-Rokem for their valuable suggestions and comments at different stages of this study.

References

Almazán, Vicente 1996: The Pilgrim-Shell in Denmark. In: M. Dunn & L. K. Davidson (eds.) *The Pilgrimage to Compostela in the Middle Ages: A Book of Essays*. New York, London: Garland.

Anderson, Benedict 1991: *Imagined Communities: Reflection on the Origin and Spread of Nationalism*. 2nd edition. London: Verso.

Anttonen, Pertti J. 2005: *Tradition through Modernity: Postmodernism and the Nation-State in Folklore Scholarship*. Helsinki: Finnish Literature Society.

Bendix, Regina 1997: *In Search of Authenticity*. Madison: University of Wisconsin Press.

Bendix, Regina & Dorothee Hemme 2004: Fairy Tale Activists: Narrative Imaginaries Along a German Tourist Route. *Tautosakos darbai* 21: 187–197.

Biella, Daniele 2003: *Convergenze tra Realtà e Communità Virtuale nel Pellegrinaggio a Santiago de Compostela*. MA Thesis, University of Bergamo. Available online at: http://dinamico.unibg.it/lazzari/santiago_de_compostela.

Coleman, Simon & John Elsner 1995: *Pilgrimage, Past and Present*. London: British Museum Press.

Coleman, Simon & John Elsner 2002: Pilgrim Voices: Authoring Christian Pilgrimage. In: S. Coleman & J. Elsner (eds.) *Pilgrim Voices: Narrative and Authorship in Christian Pilgrimage*. New York, Oxford: Berghahn.

Coleman, Simon & John Elsner 2004: Tradition as Play: Pilgrimage to "England's Nazareth". *History and Anthropology* 15: 3, 273–288.

Dunn, Maryjane & Linda Kay Davidson 1996: Bibliography of the Pilgrimage: The State of the Art. In: M. Dunn & L. K. Davidson (eds.) *The Pilgrimage to Compostela in the Middle Ages: A Book of Essays*. New York, London: Garland.

Eade, John & Michael J. Sallnow 1991: Introduction. In: J. Eade & M. J. Sallnow (eds.) *Contesting the Sacred*. London: Routledge.

Edensor, Tim 2000: Walking in the British Countryside: Reflexivity, Embodied Practices and Ways to Escape. *Body & Society* 6: 81–106.

Frey, Nancy Louise 1998: *Pilgrim Stories: On and Off the

Road to Santiago. Berkley, Los Angeles: University of California Press.

Gower, Kathy 2002: *Incorporating a Hero's Journey: A Modern Day Pilgrimage on the Camino de Santiago*. PhD dissertation, California Institute of Integral Studies.

Hills, Matt 2002: *Fan Cultures*. London, New York: Routledge.

Hobsbawm, Eric 1983: Introduction. In: E. Hobsbawm & T. Ranger (eds.) *The Invention of Tradition*. Cambridge: Cambridge University Press.

Johler, Reinhard 2002: Local Europe. The Production of Cultural Heritage and the Europeanisation of Places. *Ethnologia Europaea* 32: 7–18.

Kirshenblatt-Gimblett, Barbara 1995: Theorizing Heritage. *Ethnomusicology* 39: 3, 367–380.

Kirshenblatt-Gimblett, Barbara 2005: From Ethnology to Heritage. *Proceedings of the SIEF conference – Marseille 2004*. Available on-line at: http://www.nyu.edu/classes/bkg/web/SIEF.pdf.

Lois González, Rubén Camilo & José Somoza Medina 2003: Cultural Tourism and Urban Management in Northwestern Spain: The Pilgrimage to Santiago de Compostela. *Tourism Geographies* 5: 4, 446–460.

Macauley, David 2001: Walking the Elemental Earth: Phenomenological and Literary "Foot Notes". *Analecta Husserliana* 71, 15–31.

MacWilliams, Mark 2002: Virtual Pilgrimages on the Internet. *Religion* 32: 315–335.

Matsura, Kioshin 2004: Preface. *Museum International* 56: 1–2, 4–5.

Mayol, Antoinette (ed.) 2004: *Collection Vers Comostelle*. Toulouse: Editions ACIR.

Moulin, Claude & Priscilla Boniface 2001: Routeing Heritage for Tourism: Making Heritage and Cultural Tourism Networks for Socio-economic Development. *International Journal for Heritage Studies* 7: 3, 237–248.

Murray, Michael & Brian Graham 1997: Exploring the Dialectics of Route-Based Tourism: The Camino de Santiago. *Tourism Management*. 18. 8, 513–524.

Ó Giolláin, Diarmuid 2000: *Locating Irish Folklore: Tradition, Modernity, Identity*. Cork: Cork University Press.

Peake, Harold 1919: Santiago: The Evolution of a Patron Saint. *Folklore* 30: 3, 208–226.

Péricard-Méa, Denise 2000: *Compostelle et Cultes de Saint Jacques au Moyen Age*. Paris: Presses Universitaires de France.

Scollon, Ron & Suzie Wong-Scollon 2003: *Discourses in Place: Language in the Material World*. London, New York: Routledge.

Slavin, Sean 2003: Walking as a Spiritual Practice: The Pilgrimage to Santiago de Compostela. *Body & Society*. 9: 3, 1–18.

Stockstad, Marilyn 1978: *Santiago de Compostela in the Age of the Great Pilgrimage*. Norman Ok.: University of Oklahoma Press.

Thomas-Penette, Michel 2000: Cultural Routes of the Council of Europe: From the Garden to the Landscape. *Campaign Diary*. European Institute of Cultural Routes.

UNESCO 2005: *Operational Guidelines for the Implementation of the World Heritage Convention*, available at the Unesco World Heritage Center Website, http://whc.unesco.org/archive/opguide05-en.pdf. Accessed 20.11.2006.

Wylie, John 2005: A Single Day's Walking: Narrating Self and Landscape on the South West Coast Path. *Transactions Institute of British Geographers* 30: 234–247.

Dani Schrire is a PhD candidate in the Jewish and Comparative Folklore Program at the Hebrew University of Jerusalem. His dissertation focuses on the attitude of Zionist folklorists in the 1940s–50s to Jewish life in exile and is part of a broader project on disciplinary history of cultural studies carried out by the Hebrew University together with Georg August Universität in Göttingen.
(dani.schrire@mail.huji.ac.il)